Das ist Deutsch!

A Photocopiable German Language Scheme for Primary Schools

Kathy Williams and Amanda Doyle

Brilliant Publications

Publisher's information

Published by Brilliant Publications
Unit 10,
Sparrow Hall Farm,
Edlesborough,
Dunstable,
Bedfordshire,
LU6 2ES

Sales and stock enquiries:
Tel: 01202 712910
Fax: 0845 1309300
e-mail: brilliant@bebc.co.uk
website: www.brilliantpublications.co.uk

General information enquiries:
Tel: 01525 222292

The name 'Brilliant Publications' and the logo are registered trade marks.

Written by Kathy Williams and Amanda Doyle
Illustrated by Chantel Kees
Cover illustration by Linda Murray
Printed in the UK
© Kathy Williams and Amanda Doyle
ISBN 978-1-905780-15-0
First published 2008
10 9 8 7 6 5 4 3 2 1

Introduction

Das ist Deutsch! is designed for non-specialist teachers of foreign languages. The scheme aims to encourage primary-school pupils to enjoy learning German, and to communicate in speech and writing through the acquisition of simple grammar and a variety of vocabulary.

Each of the 18 units has teachers' notes and photocopiable pupil worksheets. Each unit addresses several learning objectives, allowing for the material to be taught over several lessons or as a whole. Grammar teaching is approached through the context of the unit theme, for example 'der'/'die'/'das' in the context of household objects and adjectives in the unit about clothes. There is progression through the units, but they can equally be selected for use in a different order, to complement classwork in maths or English, for example.

The 'Schlüsselwörter – Key Words' section in the teachers' notes for each unit contains the language that pupils should learn. Frequent references are made to relevant units elsewhere in the book where the same key language also appears. Additional vocabulary may be required to meet pupils' particular interests, and some of the activities require the use of a German–English dictionary.

The 'Activities' sections are written as suggested lessons and provide readily accessible teaching plans that can be adapted and altered to suit individual needs. The 'Further activities' are not always more difficult; they provide further suggested ways of working within the unit if more time is available, and include ideas for successful classroom displays, as well as larger group or whole-school exercises. All the worksheets may be adapted and modified to suit individual pupils. Several are designed to be cut up to make flashcards or games. These sheets would benefit from enlargement and/or lamination.

The 'Grammar Points' section includes notes on basic grammar concepts introduced in the units. A complete listing of the 'Schlüsselwörter – Key Words' is on pages 104–108.

Many opportunities exist to link the study of German language through Das ist Deutsch! to other curriculum areas: literacy and numeracy, ICT, technology, geography, music, art and sport. Pupils can collaborate with others in pairs and groups and expand their cultural awareness. Above all, pupils can experience through learning a foreign language a sense of personal achievement that they can carry forward into their secondary-school language learning.

Contents

Guten Tag

Learning objectives

Pupils will be able to:

* Say hello and introduce themselves
* Greet people
* Use the alphabet in German

Resources needed

* Sheets 1a, 1b, 1c
* German name cards.

Activities

* Introduce 'Guten Tag'. Pupils repeat the word. You could move around the class and shake hands with individuals saying 'Guten Tag,' encouraging them to reply. Explain greeting customs: shaking hands, kissing on both cheeks.

* Introduce 'Wie heißt du?' for recognition, and reply 'Ich heiße … '. On Sheet 1a pupils can fill in their picture frame and copy the sentences.

* Introduce the phrases 'Wie geht's?' and 'Gut, danke.' Pupils repeat the question and answer. They could question each other and give the response.

* Introduce 'Auf Wiedersehen.' Pupils repeat it. Mix with 'Guten Tag' to practise.

* Distribute cards from sheet 1b. Pupils say the word or phrase that they have on their card. Work together to build up a dialogue by putting the phrases into a logical sequence. Sheet 1c gives a completed dialogue.

* Read out the alphabet in German. Spell the name of someone in the class in German – the first person to guess the name correctly wins a point. Play in teams. Pupils could take the role of caller.

* Pupils spell out their own names for a partner to write exactly as they say. They could use German name cards for additional practice.

Further activities

* Give each pupil a card with a 'new' German name. They introduce themselves using 'Ich heiße … ' (see sheet 6a for sample names).

* Pupils 'meet' each other around the group using as many phrases as possible in a conversation (with or without reference to sheet 1c). The question 'Wie heißt du?' could be incorporated into the dialogues.

* Using photographs, pupils mount their picture with 'Guten Tag. Ich heiße … ' beneath it, round it etc. Make a class display.

Schlüsselwörter – Key words

Guten Tag	hello
Auf Wiedersehen	goodbye
Ich heiße …	My name is …
Wie geht's?	How are you?
Gut, danke	Fine, thank you
danke	thank you
Wie heißt du?	What is your name?

Das ist Deutsch!

Guten Tag

Hello

Guten Tag.
Ich heiße Anna.

Guten Tag.
Ich heiße Moritz.

Zeichne dich selbst und schreibe
die Sätze ab:

Draw yourself and copy the sentences:

_____   _____

_____   _____

_____

Das ist Deutsch!
www.brilliantpublications.co.uk

Sag

Say

✂

sag:

Hello

say:

sag:

How are you?

say:

sag:

I'm very well

say:

sag:

Thank you

say:

sag:

My name is ...

say:

sag:

Goodbye

say:

Das ist Deutsch!   © Kathy Williams and Amanda Doyle

Ein Gespräch

Das ist Deutsch!

In der Klasse

Learning objectives

Pupils will be able to:

* Understand and use some classroom instructions and language
* Name some common school equipment

Resources needed

* Sheets 2a, 2b
* School equipment (eg pencil, pen, ruler), cloth/tea towel, tray.

Activities

* Use mime and gestures for each of the verbs (as applicable) from the Schlüsselwörter, encouraging pupils to name (in German) the relevant verb. Say 'Sehr gut' after each correct response.

* Introduce the phrase 'Es tut mir leid'. There are opportunities to practise its use later in the Unit.

* You could give a series of instructions for a game of 'Simon sagt'. Just as in 'Simon says', the pupils should respond only if you say 'Simon sagt' in front of the instructions.

* Pupils could choose one or more of the instructions to design as a poster for classroom reference.

* Pupils will see examples of instructions that they will come across in the course on sheet 2a.

* Introduce the names of objects

Schlüsselwörter – Key words

setzen, bitte	sit down, please (whole class)
setz dich, bitte	sit down, please (one child)
aufstehen	to stand up
höre zu	to listen
schau hin	to watch/look
sprecht mir nach	say after me (whole class)
sprich mir nach	say after me (one child)
ausfüllen	to fill in
machen	to do
verbinden	to join
abschreiben	to copy
(vor)lesen	to read (out)
zeichnen	to draw
beantworten	to answer
fertig machen	to complete/finish
schreiben	to write
finden	to find
sehr gut	very good
es tut mir leid	I'm sorry
ja	yes
nein	no
das ist	it is/this is
der Bleistift	pencil
der Kugelschreiber	pen
die Tasche	bag
das Heft	exercise book
der Bleistiftspitzer	sharpener
das Lineal	ruler
der Radiergummi	eraser
die Federmäppchen	pencil case
Was heißt das auf Deutsch?	What is this in German?

Das ist Deutsch!

used in the classroom (see Schlüsselwörter) by placing a variety of school equipment (pen, pencil etc) on a tray or desk. Pick items up and say 'Das ist ein Kugelschreiber' (or whatever); pupils repeat if the object is 'ein Kugelschreiber' or correct you if it is not. Use 'Ja, das ist ein Kugelschreiber' or 'Nein, das ist ein ... '. You could explain here the use of the indefinite article ein/eine. It is dealt with further in Unit 5 (see Grammar Points).

✳ Cover the equipment on the tray with a cloth and remove one item from underneath. The pupils must guess which is missing once the cloth is removed.

✳ A matching game is on sheet 2b; pupils have to write the names of items used at school.

✳ Explain to the pupils that 'Es tut mir leid' can be used if you do not have something. Use 'Es tut mir leid' with 'Ich habe keinen Bleistift' (I don't have a pencil) etc. Encourage the pupils to question each other.

✳ Play a version of 'The Generation Game' final memory game. Pupils watch as a series of school items is shown (moving conveyor belt not compulsory!). One pupil then volunteers to say them in the order that they appeared. To make it harder, items may appear more than once in the sequence. Start off with a few items, introducing further items as the pupils get more confident.

Further activities

✳ Pupils could label further items around the room, eg die Tür = the door, das Fenster = the window, die Tafel = the black/white board. Encourage use of the phrase 'Was heißt das auf Deutsch?' to find German translations for English words.

✳ Pupils could use 'Das gehört mir' = 'That belongs to me.' Collect pencils and books from the pupils, and hold each item up separately for the children to name. The pupil who owns the item says: 'Das gehört mir.'

Im Klassenzimmer

In the classroom

Die Lücken | ausfüllen | _____ the gaps.

Die Namen | schreiben | _____ the names.

Verbinden

 Phil

Die Tiere mit den Wörter verbinden:

ein Fisch (m)

eine Katze (f)

Zuhören _____

Die CD anhören.

Beantworten _____

Die Fragen beantworten.
Hast du einen Freund? Ja.

Lesen _____

Die Passage lesen.

Ausfüllen _____

Die Liste ausfüllen.

1, 2, __ , 4, 5, __ .

Zeichnen _____

Ein Haus zeichnen.

Finden _____

Die Wörter 'Guten' und 'Tag' finden.

G	U	T	E	N	O	E
A	X	O	E	C	B	T
B	O	N	J	O	U	A
G	B	E	K	D	F	G

Das ist Deutsch!   © Kathy Williams and Amanda Doyle

Meine Schulsachen

My things at school

Wer hat welche Sache?
Who has which thing?

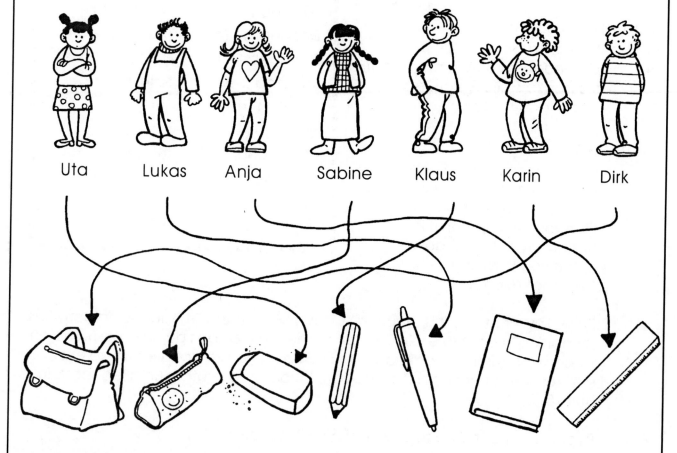

Uta   Lukas   Anja   Sabine   Klaus   Karin   Dirk

Beende die Sätze:

Complete the sentences:

Uta hat _____ . *Uta has*

Lukas hat _____ .

Anja hat _____ .

Sabine hat _____ .

Klaus hat _____ .

Karin hat _____ .

Dirk hat _____ .

| einen Bleistift | ein Federmäppchen | einen Radiergummi | ein Heft |
| ein Lineal | einen Kugelschreiber | eine Tasche | |

Das ist Deutsch!

www.brilliantpublications.co.uk

Die Woche

Learning objectives

Pupils will be able to:

✳ Recognize and use days of the week

Resources needed

✳ Sheets 3a, 3b

✳ Calendar; card; A4 transparent file pockets; sticky notelets or paper and Blu-tack

Activities

✳ Introduce the days of the week (pointing at days on a calendar as you say their names in German). In German it is customary to list the days of the week starting with 'Montag' (Monday).

✳ Pupils say what day it is 'heute' ('today'). Continue with suggested activities for particular days to elicit German name: eg perhaps pupils have music on Tuesday or swimming on Friday. You could mime the activities: there may be several correct answers! Activities are introduced in other units, eg sports in Unit 15.

✳ Pupils fill in sheet 3a with a typical activity for each day.

Further activities

✳ Pupils mime activities for partner to guess the day.

✳ Pupils could make a weekly reminder board to take home (photocopy sheet 3b onto A4-size paper or card). The day boxes could be illustrated/ decorated. Put the A4 paper/card into a transparent pocket. Sticky notelets or paper with Blu-tack can be used to put messages/reminders onto relevant days. At the end of the week the plan is reusable! An alternative design would be to use a cork tile. Stick or write the days of the week on the tile and pin messages as required.

Schlüsselwörter – Key words	
Montag (m)	Monday
Dienstag (m)	Tuesday
Mittwoch (m)	Wednesday
Donnerstag (m)	Thursday
Freitag (m)	Friday
Samstag (m)	Saturday
Sonntag (m)	Sunday
die Tage (m pl)	the days
die Woche	the week
die Tage der Woche	the days of the week
heute	today

Das ist Deutsch!

© Kathy Williams and Amanda Doyle

Die Tage der Woche

The days of the week

Zeichne was du jeden Tag machst.

Draw something that you do each day.

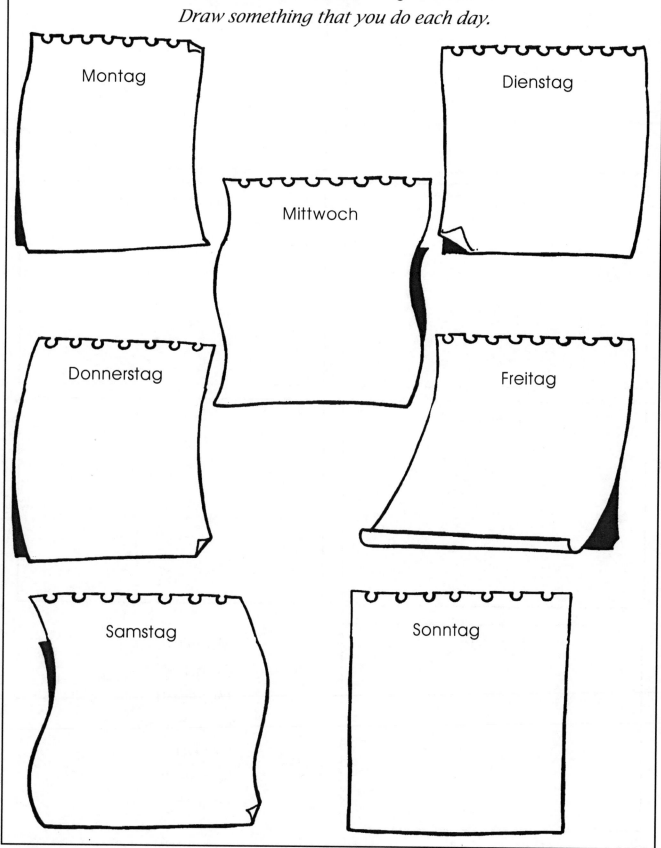

Montag

Dienstag

Mittwoch

Donnerstag

Freitag

Samstag

Sonntag

Das ist Deutsch!

www.brilliantpublications.co.uk

Die Tage der Woche

The days of the week

Montag	Dienstag
Mittwoch	Donnerstag
Freitag	Samstag

Sonntag

Montag
Dienstag
Mittwoch
Donnerstag
Freitag
Samstag
Sonntag

www.brilliantpublications.co.uk **Das ist Deutsch!**

Die Jahreszeiten/das Wetter

Learning objectives

Pupils will be able to:

* Talk about the weather and seasons in general
* Describe the day's weather conditions

Resources needed

* Sheets 4a, 4b, 4c, 4d
* Cardboard; split pins; large sheet of paper; sticky notelets or paper and Blu-tack.

Activities

* Introduce weather expressions. Show the flashcards (sheet 4a), naming the seasons and conditions. Pupils repeat the phrases.

* Use the flashcards to emphasize weather expressions. Place flashcards in a row face down on a table/board. One pupil picks a card, gives it to you without looking at it and has a guess at the weather expression. If incorrect, then the other members of the group can guess. The correct pupil chooses another card, and so on.

* Pupils fill in the weather wheel (sheet 4b) by putting the correct phrase(s) with the pictures. They could mount it on cardboard and put a split pin through the middle with the arrow cut out. Highlight repetition of 'Es ist ...'

* Introduce the question 'Wie ist das Wetter heute?' Pupils move the arrow to point to today's weather and respond. They could also point and say the weather for other days as if they were back on that day.

* Introduce seasons by asking 'Wie ist das Wetter im Herbst/im Winter?' Suggest several typical weather conditions to help elicit understanding of season words. Repeat, eg 'Im Herbst es ist windig und es regnet.' Pupils suggest weather typical of each season.

* Sheet 4c can be used to reinforce the seasons.

* Sheet 4d. This exercise combines the seasons and the weather. Pupils choose a correct phrase and write it beneath the appropriate picture.

Schlüsselwörter – Key words

im Frühling	in spring
im Sommer	in summer
im Herbst	in autumn
im Winter	in winter
es regnet	it rains/is raining
es schneit	it snows/is snowing
es ist schön	it is fine
es ist sonnig	it is sunny
es ist schrecklich	it is horrible
es ist heiß	it is hot
es ist kalt	it is cold
es ist windig	it is windy
Wie ist das Wetter?	What is the weather like?
heute	today

Further activities

✳ Pupils could use a chart similar to 'Die Woche' week plan (Unit 3) to record the weather each day for a week either by writing the phrase or drawing a weather symbol. On Friday you could review the week's weather.

✳ Weather 'round-up'. Draw a large outline of Germany on the board/large sheet of paper. Mark on a few principal towns, eg Berlin, Köln, Frankfurt, München etc (sheet 6b could be enlarged). Pupils prepare weather symbols in pairs/groups on sticky notelets or small pieces of paper and Blu-tack. They then present a weather 'round-up' saying 'In Berlin regnet es' or 'In Köln ist es schön' etc while sticking their symbols on the map.

Das ist Deutsch! © Kathy Williams and Amanda Doyle

Das Wetter – Karten

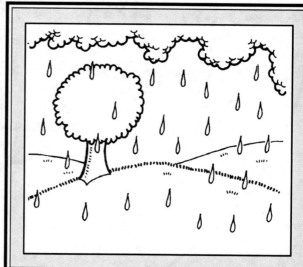

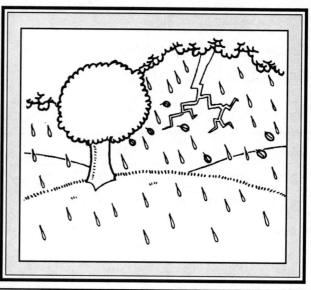

Das ist Deutsch!

www.brilliantpublications.co.uk

Wie ist das Wetter heute?

What is the weather like today?

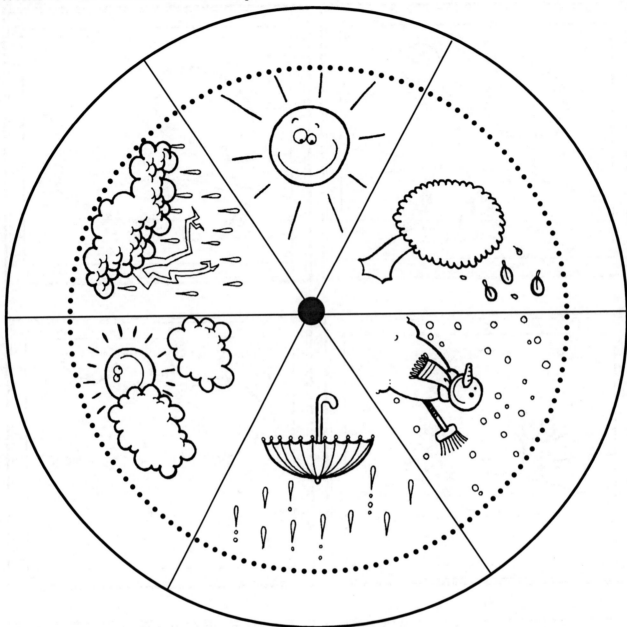

Finde den richtigen Satz.

Find the right sentence.

es regnet	es schneit
es ist schön	es ist sonnig
es ist schrecklich	es ist heiß
es ist kalt	es ist windig

Schneide den Pfeil aus und mache ihn in der Mitte fest.

Cut out the arrow and put it in the middle.

Das ist Deutsch!

Die Jahreszeiten

The seasons

Zeichne etwas für jede Jahreszeit.
Draw something for each season.

der Frühling

der Sommer

der Herbst

der Winter

Das ist Deutsch!

www.brilliantpublications.co.uk

Wie ist das Wetter im Sommer?

What is the weather like in summer?

Schreibe den passenden Satz unter jedes Bild.

Write the correct sentence under each picture.

Choose from:

Im Winter ist es kalt	Im Herbst regnet es	Im Frühling regnet es
Im Sommer ist es heiß	Im Winter schneit es	Im Sommer ist es sonnig
	Im Herbst ist es windig	Im Frühling ist es schön

Das ist Deutsch!

Die Zahlen 1–20

Learning objectives

Pupils will be able to:

✳ Count to 20

✳ Recognize the use of ein/eine instead of eins when referring directly to a noun – masculine and neuter (ein)/feminine (eine)

Resources needed

✳ Sheets 5a, 5b, 5c

✳ Pencils, sweets, toys, bricks, etc for counting; hat.

Activities

Part A

✳ Practise repeating numbers 1–10. Pupils could use fingers to count and repeat.

✳ Using 10 pencils, sweets or toys, ask pupils in turn to hand you something, eg 'Geben Sie mir drei Bleistifte, bitte.' When a pupil has chosen the correct number of pencils, return them to the set and start again. Divide pupils into groups and let them ask the questions. Note: For a single person, use 'Gib mir drei Bleistifte, bitte.'

Schlüsselwörter – Key words	
eins	1
zwei	2
drei	3
vier	4
fünf	5
sechs	6
sieben	7
acht	8
neun	9
zehn	10
elf	11
zwölf	12
dreizehn	13
vierzehn	14
fünfzehn	15
sechzehn	16
siebzehn	17
achtzehn	18
neunzehn	19
zwanzig	20
ein/eine	one/a/an
bitte geben Sie mir/ gib mir	please give me

✳ Use sheets 5a and 5b together.
Cut 5a into 10 separate cards. Pupils can then stick the written numbers over the grid. Highlight the 'ts' sound made by the letter z.

Part B

✳ Practise repeating numbers 11–16. Highlight the 'ts' sound made by the letter z.

✳ Give each pupil a number between 11 and 20. Ask all the pupils to stand up to start the game. As you say a number, the pupils repeat it and sit down if it is their number. The winner(s) are those left standing at the end. Note: Point out that 6 (sechs) loses its 's' and 7 (sieben) loses its 'en' when 'zehn' is added.

✳ Show pupils three, then four etc, items (sweets etc), or use fingers, then add 'plus' (pronounced 'ploos') 10. This allows highlighting of the numbers 13–19 as dreizehn, vierzehn etc.

✳ Sheet 5c can be used to reinforce all the numbers. Highlight how the number one can be 'ein' or 'eine' because words are either masculine, feminine or neuter (see Grammar Notes). You could refer pupils back to school equipment (sheet 2b) to check understanding.

Further activities

✳ Using the question 'Wieviel … gibt es im Klassenzimmer?', ask pupils to count items in the classroom to give a numerical response.

✳ Play 'Loto'. Pupils draw a noughts-and-crosses grid and choose numbers 1–20 to put on it. Call out numbers from a hat (you or a pupil); the pupils cross them out as they hear them. The winner is the first to have all nine numbers crossed out and to have called 'Loto!'

✳ Make up mathematical sums and ask pupils to give the solution in German. Here are some examples:

English	German	Pronounced	Sum in words	In numbers
add	plus	ploos	zehn plus drei	10 + 3
subtract	minus	me noos	elf minus sieben	11 – 7
multiply by	mal	maal	zwei mal fünf	2 x 5
divide by	geteilt durch	gtile t doorch	zwölf geteilt durch sechs	12 ÷ 6
equals	gleich	gl eye ch	drei mal zwei gleich sechs	3 x 2 = 6

✳ Use the grid on sheet 5b as number flashcards for a simple game. Give each pupil a number card and call out a number at random. The pupil with that card has to stand up and call another number. This continues until all pupils are standing; the last one to stand up is the winner.

Das ist Deutsch!　　© Kathy Williams and Amanda Doyle

Die Zahlen 1–10

Numbers 1-10

vier

sieben

zehn

eins

zwei

fünf

sechs

acht

neun

drei

Das ist Deutsch!

www.brilliantpublications.co.uk

Tafel der Zahlen

Number grid

1	2
3	4
5	6
7	8
9	10

Number grid

Das ist Deutsch!

© Kathy Williams and Amanda Doyle

Bis zwanzig zählen

Count to 20

Zähle und fülle die Lücken aus.
Count and fill in the blanks.

Remember: Words can be either feminine, masculine or neuter. The word for banana is a feminine word, so we add an 'e' onto the end of 'ein'.

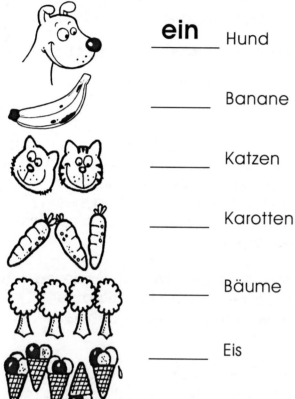

ein _____ Hund

_____ Banane

_____ Katzen

_____ Karotten

_____ Bäume

_____ Eis

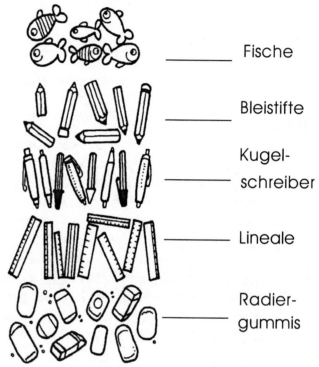

_____ Fische

_____ Bleistifte

_____ Kugel-schreiber

_____ Lineale

_____ Radier-gummis

Verbinde die Zahlen mit dem englischen Wort:

Match the numbers to the English:

elf	thirteen
zwölf	twelve
dreizehn	eleven
vierzehn	fourteen
fünfzehn	sixteen
sechzehn	fifteen

Zähle zusammen:

Do the addition:

zehn + sieben = **siebzehn**
10   7

zehn + acht =
10   8   _____

zehn + neun =
10   9   _____

zehn + zehn =
10   10   _____

Das ist Deutsch!

Ich stelle mich vor

Learning objectives

Pupils will be able to:

* Say where they live
* Identify some town names and locations in Germany
* Say their address
* Use numbers in addresses

Resources needed

* Sheets 6a, 6b, 6c
* Map of Germany with cities, rivers, mountains, regions marked; card.

Schlüsselwörter – Key words	
Ich heiße ...	My name is ...
Wo wohnst du?	Where do you live?
Ich wohne in ...	I live in ...
Meine Adresse ist ...	My address is ...

Activities

* Display a large map of Germany (or enlarge a copy of sheet 6b) and locate the places mentioned on the top of sheet 6a onto the map. Give each pupil a character picture cut from 6a (match pupils' genders). Ask pupils to decide where in Germany they'd like their character to live, and they respond as their character saying 'Ich heiße ... ' and 'Ich wohne in ... '. Stick characters and town names on the map together.

* Introduce 'Wo wohnst du?' Pupils answer using their own town name, eg 'Ich wohne in Reading.' You could extend practice by using the character pictures along with the cut-out town names. You could revise 'Ich heiße ... ' at the same time.

* Introduce 'Meine Adresse ist ... ' Pupils use numbers (see Unit 5) to say their address if it includes a house number (for numbers 20+, refer to Units 8 and 14).

* Ask pupils to fill in sheet 6c. See if they can work out the meaning of the question at the bottom of the sheet. 'Das Haus' is the theme of the next unit. You could talk about how many German people live in flats or 'Wohnungen' in cities .

Further activities

* Look at a map of Germany and identify additional main towns and cities. You could locate other principal geographical landmarks such as rivers (der Rhein, die Donau, die Elbe, die Mosel and der Main), die Nordsee-Küste, der Schwarzwald, die Alpen and the rolling volcanic landscape of the Eifel to the east. You could extend this to a study of one of these landmarks/areas. Have any of the pupils visited Germany?

* Give pupils cards with a 'new' address, including a 'new' town. Ask them 'Wo wohnst du?' and 'Was ist deine Adresse?' Alternatively, prompt pupils to ask each other and answer using 'Ich wohne in ... ', 'Meine Adresse ist ... '.

Das ist Deutsch! © Kathy Williams and Amanda Doule

Die Leute (Karten)

- Leipzig
- Berlin
- Stuttgart
- Frankfurt
- München
- Bonn
- Hamburg
- Hannover

Hans

Anna

Sabine

Moritz

Karin

Lukas

Klaus

Uta

Das ist Deutsch!

Ich stelle mich vor

I'd like to introduce myself

Wählt aus, wer in welcher Stadt lebt.
Choose who lives in which city.

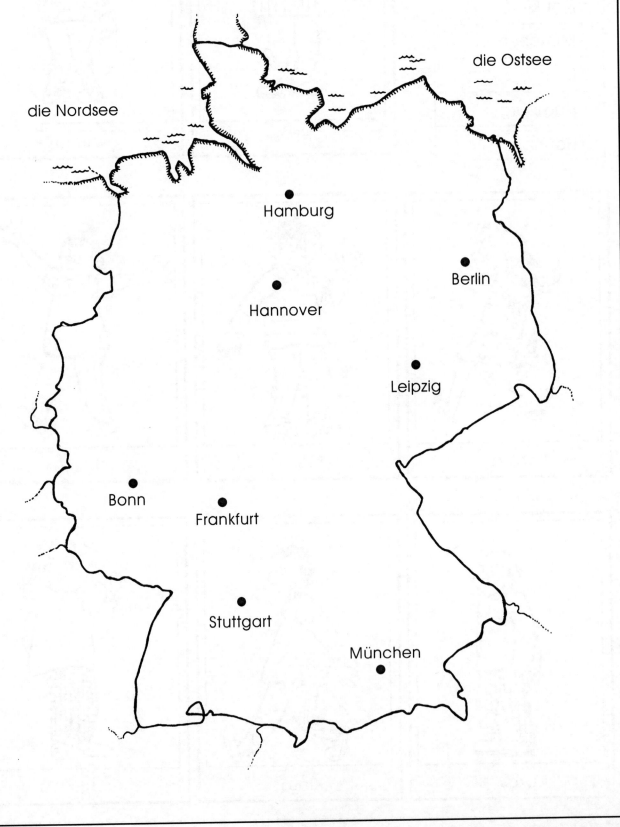

die Ostsee

die Nordsee

Hamburg

Berlin

Hannover

Leipzig

Bonn

Frankfurt

Stuttgart

München

Das ist Deutsch!

Wo wohnst du?

Where do you live?

Beantworte die Fragen.
Answer the questions.

Meine Adresse ist

SINGERSTRASSE 8

1000 BERLIN

PAR AVION

Karl Braun
Singerstrasse 8
1000 Berlin
Germany

Was ist deine Adresse?

_____

Wo wohnst du?

_____

Wohnst du in einem Haus
oder einer Wohnung?

_____

Das ist Deutsch!

www.brilliantpublications.co.uk

Zu Hause

Learning objectives

Pupils will be able to:

✱ Say what rooms are in their house, using 'Es gibt … '
✱ Say which room someone is 'in'
✱ Recognize the use of der/die/das as the definite article 'the' with masculine/feminine/neuter words
✱ Say what is in their bedroom

Resources needed

✱ Sheets 7a, 7b, 7c
✱ Pictures of rooms cut from magazines.

Activities

✱ Using sheet 7a as flash cards, introduce room words.

✱ Hide a single card behind a larger card and slowly reveal a part of it. Pupils guess which room is appearing.

✱ Mime activities relating to each room. Pupils guess the room. They could do this in pairs or as a group.

Schlüsselwörter – Key words	
die Küche	kitchen
das Wohnzimmer	living room
das Schlafzimmer	bedroom
die Diele	hall
das Badezimmer	bathroom
die Garage	garage
das Esszimmer	dining room
der Dachboden	loft
der Keller	cellar
der (masculine)	the
die (feminine)	the
das (neuter)	the
in	in
Es gibt …	there is/are (plus accusative)
das Bett	bed
der Teppich	rug
der Kleiderschrank	wardrobe
die Tisch	table
der Stuhl	chair
Wo ist … ?	Where is … ?

✱ Highlight der/die/das; all mean 'the'. Group the words into those that are feminine (die), those that are neuter (das) and those that are masculine (der) – see Schlüsselwörter. (For more information, see Grammar Points.)

✱ Give a description of a house using 'In meinem Haus gibt es … '. Ask pupils to describe their own houses.

✱ Introduce the question 'Wo ist … ?' Read the questions on sheet 7b and allow pupils to answer orally (then in writing if required) to practise room words. (Note that we are using dative 'im' for masculine and neuter words, and 'in der' for feminine words.)

Das ist Deutsch! © *Kathy Williams and Amanda Doyle*

✳   Sheet 7c introduces some common bedroom furniture words. Pupils could design a bedroom by cutting out the furniture and positioning it on the plan. They could use a dictionary to look up the German words for further items and include them as well.

✳   They could present their finished plans describing their bedrooms using 'In meinem Schlafzimmer gibt es … ' (for use of 'some', refer to Unit 14).

Further activities

✳   Using cut-out pictures from magazines, pupils could mount their pictures on a page, labelling the rooms 'die Küche', 'das Schlafzimmer' etc. They could title the page 'Zu Verkaufen' (for sale) and make a house particulars sheet from an imaginary 'Immobilienmakler' (Estate Agent). A picture of the exterior of a house could complete the advertisement.

✳   Make a display board with 'adverts' framed to look like an agency window.

Zu Hause

In the house

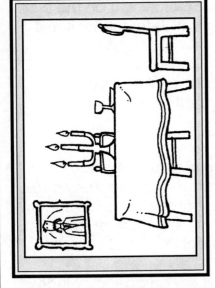
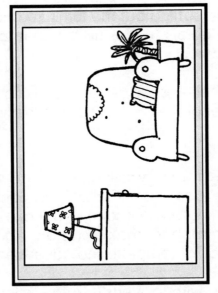
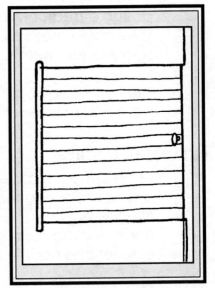

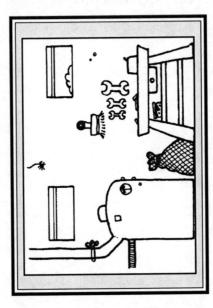
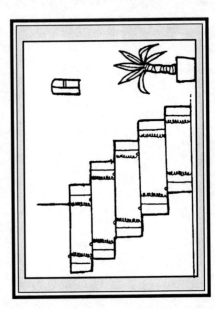

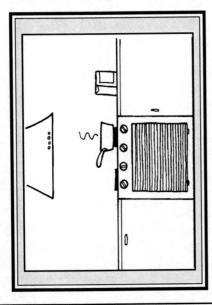
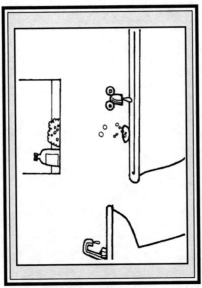

Das ist Deutsch!

© Kathy Williams and Amanda Doyle

Wo ist Hans?

Where is Hans?

Beantworte die Fragen und fülle die Lücken aus.
Answer the questions and fill in the gaps.

Wo ist Hans?   Im   **Schlafzimmer**

Wo ist Sofie?   Im   _____

Wo ist Mutti?   Im   _____

Wo ist Vati?   In der   _____

Wo ist Lukas?   Im   _____

Wo ist der Hund?   In der   _____

Wo ist die Katze?   In der   _____

Wo ist die Spinne?   Im   _____

Wo ist die Maus?   Auf dem   _____

Das ist Deutsch!

www.brilliantpublications.co.uk

Im meinem Schlafzimmer

In my bedroom

Hier ist ein Plan von deinem Schlafzimmer.
Here is a plan of your bedroom.

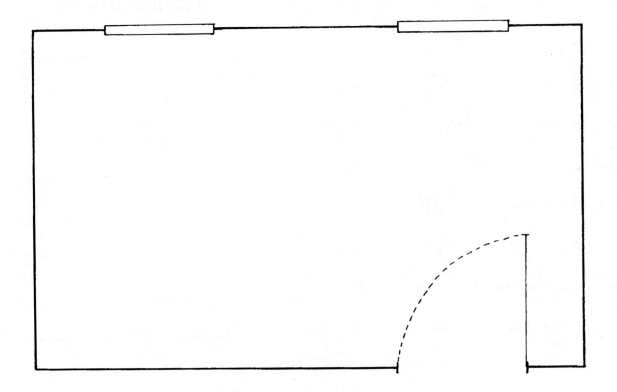

Schneide die Möbel aus und setze Sie auf den Plan.
Cut out the furniture and put it on the plan.

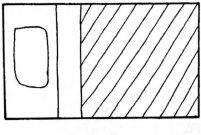

ein Bett

ein Stuhl

ein Tisch

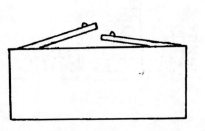

ein Kleiderschrank

ein Teppich

Das ist Deutsch!   © Kathy Williams and Amanda Doyle

Wann hast du Geburtstag?

Learning objectives

Pupils will be able to:

* Say the months of the year
* Say when their birthday is
* Recognize some special holidays and learn about their significance
* Say how old they are
* Use numbers to 31

Resources needed

* Sheets 8a, 8b, 8c, 8d, 8e.
* Pictures from magazines/ photographs/book illustrations showing different weather conditions; glitter; glue; card/ paper.

Activities

* Using a variety of weather pictures (or sheet 4a flashcards), elicit suitable months for each (in German if possible, or English to start).

* Practise pronunciation of the months. Pupils match illustrations with names of months on sheet 8a.

* Pupils suggest months for various activities: holidays, skiing, New Year, at school etc.

* Introduce the question 'Wann hast du Geburtstag?' Pupils say which month their birthday is in, eg 'im März'.

* Revise numbers 1 to 20 (Unit 5). Continue with the numbers 21 to 31. Pupils use the appropriate number to say when the date of their birthday is, eg 'am siebzehnten Februar'.

Schlüsselwörter – Key words

Januar (m)	January
Februar (m)	February
März (m)	March
April (m)	April
Mai (m)	May
Juni (m)	June
Juli (m)	July
August (m)	August
September (m)	September
Oktober (m)	October
November (m)	November
Dezember (m)	December
die Monate des Jahres	the months of the year
der Feiertag	holiday
das Weihnachten	Christmas
das Ostern	Easter
das Silvester	New Year's Eve
das Neujahr	New Year
Wie alt bist du?	How old are you?
Ich bin … Jahre alt	I'm … years old
Fröhliche Weihnachten!	Merry Xmas!
Ein gutes neues Jahr!	Happy New Year!
Frohe Ostern!	Happy Easter!
Alles Gute zum Geburtstag!	Happy Birthday!
Mein Geburtstag ist …	My birthday is …
der Muttertag	Mother's Day
der Vatertag	Father's Day
einundzwanzig	twenty-one
zweiundzwanzig	twenty-two
dreiundzwanzig	twenty-three
vierundzwanzig	twenty-four
fünfundzwanzig	twenty-five
sechsundzwanzig	twenty-six
siebenundzwanzig	twenty-seven
achtundzwanzig	twenty-eight
neunundzwanzig	twenty-nine
dreißig	thirty
einunddreißig	thirty-one
-ten/-sten	-th/-rd/-nd

✱ Introduce how to say age: 'Ich bin ... Jahre alt' in response to the question 'Wie alt bist du?' Pupils can complete sheet 8b for reinforcement.

✱ Explain that 'Happy Birthday' is usually sung in English (see sheet 8b).

✱ Prepare a set of cards/papers that have either nothing or 'heute' (today) written on them. Ask pupils to choose a card. If they pick a blank card, move to the next pupil. The pupil who chooses a 'heute' card says 'Heute habe ich Geburtstag!' The pupil makes up how old he/she is and says this in German.

✱ Talk about Christmas and other celebrations in Germany. In the Roman Catholic areas of Germany and Austria, 'Sankt Nikolaus' still comes in his bishop's robes on 6th December. However, today in many parts of Germany, he looks more like Father Christmas, and is associated with Christmas as opposed to St Nicholas Day. Pupils could find out more about how other special occasions are celebrated in Germany.

✱ Pupils could make Christmas/Easter/Mother's Day cards with greetings in German.

✱ Sheet 8c is the German song 'Oh Tannenbaum'. Pupils will recognize the tune. In English, this song is called 'Oh Christmas Tree'.

✱ Use the word search on sheet 8d to practise and revise the months, holidays and celebrations, days of the week and seasons.

✱ On Sheet 8e pupils need to work out which words match which pictures.

Further activities

✱ Pupils could find out the birthdays of famous people and report them to the group.

✱ They could write their own word search containing months/celebrations. They could put these into Christmas cards for friends in the group or other friends/family.

✱ Pupils could cut potato prints in the shape of a Christmas tree, snowman, star, present etc to make a Christmas card/poster/wrapping paper/tree decoration.

Das ist Deutsch!   © Kathy Williams and Amanda Doyle

Die Monate des Jahres

The months of the year

Verbinde die Monate mit den Bildern.

Match the months with the pictures.

Januar	August	Juni	Dezember
Februar	September	April	Oktober
November	März	Juli	Mai

Das ist Deutsch!

Wann hast du Geburtstag?

When is your birthday?

Ich habe Geburtstag!

Schreibe die Sätze ab.

Copy the sentences.

Er ist im Februar.   ____ ____ ___ _____.

Er ist am siebzehnten Februar.   ____ ___ ____ _____

_____.

Und auch für deinen Geburtstag ...

And as for your birthday as well ...

Ich bin zehn Jahre alt.

Wie alt bist du?

Das ist Deutsch!   © Kathy Williams and Amanda Doyle

Oh Tannenbaum

Oh Christmas Tree

Singe dieses Lied.
Sing this song.

Oh Tannenbaum, oh Tannenbaum,
Wie grün sind deine Blätter!

Oh Tannenbaum, oh Tannenbaum,
Wie grün sind deine Blätter!

Du grünst nicht nur zur Sommerszeit,
Nein auch im Winter, wenn es schneit.

Oh Tannenbaum, oh Tannenbaum,
Wie grün sind deine Blätter!

Das ist Deutsch!

www.brilliantpublications.co.uk

Feiertage, Monate, Tage und Jahreszeiten

Holidays, months, days and seasons

Die Wörter verstecken sich in der Wortsuche.
The words are hidden in the wordsearch.

E	M	W	G	A	T	S	N	E	I	D	S	P	R	U
M	A	I	G	K	F	R	Ü	H	L	I	N	G	T	I
O	H	N	O	V	E	M	B	E	R	E	O	S	H	N
N	J	T	F	S	B	L	L	R	S	W	U	E	L	D
A	G	E	B	U	R	T	S	T	A	G	I	P	I	O
T	E	R	J	I	U	A	V	C	U	L	P	T	R	N
E	M	O	N	T	A	G	O	A	U	G	S	E	P	N
H	Ä	K	O	T	R	M	T	J	A	D	O	M	A	E
N	R	E	T	S	O	P	D	E	Z	E	M	B	E	R
A	Z	M	A	B	N	D	J	A	S	H	M	E	W	S
F	E	I	E	R	T	A	G	U	E	L	E	R	L	T
E	Y	F	R	E	I	T	A	G	N	L	R	L	I	A
A	M	E	V	H	C	O	W	T	T	I	M	I	E	G
R	A	U	N	A	J	A	H	R	E	S	Z	E	I	T
S	A	M	S	T	A	G	B	R	E	B	O	T	K	O
B	D	O	Y	L	S	O	N	N	T	A	G	S	O	K
N	E	T	H	C	A	N	H	I	E	W	Z	I	M	T

Monate	April	März	Dezember	November
Weihnachten	Freitag	September	Sonntag	Tag
Donnerstag	Winter	Ostern	Juni	Jahreszeit
Dienstag	Geburtstag	Mai	August	Sommer
Juli	Montag	Herbst	Frühling	Januar
Feiertag	Februar	Oktober	Mittwoch	Samstag

Das ist Deutsch!

Weihnachten!

Christmas!

Was ist das?
What is it?

die Weihnachtgans   _____

ein Rentier   _____

ein Weihnachtsbaum   **Christmas tree**

ein Schneemann   _____

ein Stern   _____

Sankt Nikolaus   _____

ein Geschenk   _____

der Weihnachtsmann   _____

     www.brilliantpublications.co.uk

Länder der Welt

Learning objectives

Pupils will be able to:

✳ Name some countries and nationalities
✳ Say their own nationality
✳ Name the colours of some flags

Resources needed

✳ Sheets 9a, 9b, 9c.
✳ Dice; flags or flag pictures; bag; selection of small coloured items; books and other sources of information on countries; maps.

Activities

✳ Give each pupil a copy of 9a. Tell them that you are going to read out what each person says. Can they tell you which country each person comes from?

✳ Assign one of the names from sheet 9a to each pupil. Go round the group at random. The pupils introduce themselves using that name and 'Ich wohne in … .' Alternatively, pupils could say where they actually live.

✳ Number the countries on sheet 9a from 1–15. Pupils play in pairs or small groups. Call out a number at random in German and invite pupils to name the corresponding country.

✳ Highlight the forms of masculine and feminine nationalities. Point out that many of the feminine nationalities are created by adding -in (eg Engländerin, Waliserin, Spanierin and Italienerin). Note the masculine/feminine forms Deutscher (Deutsche), Ire (Irin), Schotte

Schlüsselwörter – Key words

Ich wohne in …	I live in …
England (n)	England
Schottland (n)	Scotland
Irland (n)	Ireland
Nordirland (n)	Northern Ireland
Wales (n)	Wales
die Niederlande (n pl)	The Netherlands
Belgien	Belgium
Polen (n)	Poland
Dänemark (n)	Denmark
Österreich (n)	Austria
Schweiz (f)	Switzerland
Deutschland (n)	Germany
Frankreich (n)	France
Italien (n)	Italy
Spanien (n)	Spain
Ich bin …	I am …
Engländer(in)	English man
Deutscher (Deutsche)	German man
Ire (Irin)	Irish man
Schotte (Schottin)	Scottish man
Waliser(in)	Welsh man
Franzose (Französin)	French man
Spanier(in)	Spanish man
Italiener(in)	Italian man
Holländer(in)	Dutch man
Pole (Polin)	Polish man
Däne (Dänin)	Danish man
Österreicher(in)	Austrian man
Schweizer(in)	Swiss man
Welche Farbe hat … ?	What colour is … ?
die Nationalflagge	the national

Das ist Deutsch! © *Kathy Williams and Amanda Doyle*

von …	flag of …
rot	red
weiß	white
blau	blue
schwarz	black
grün	green
rosa	pink
gelb	yellow
braun	brown

(Schottin), Franzose (Französin), Pole (Polin) and Däne (Dänin).

✱ Go round the group asking pupils to say where they live and their nationality. Highlight 'Ich bin … '.

✱ Using flags/flag pictures/pupils' knowledge, ask 'Welche Farbe hat die Nationalflagge von Deutschland?' 'Sie ist schwarz, rot und gold.' Highlight use of 'sie ist', because a flag is feminine. Follow with other national flags (colours are listed in Schlüsselwörter). Use sheet 9b for reinforcement; pupils could colour the flags.

✱ Give pupils a selection of coloured items. They state the colour and place the item into a bag. When you have collected all the items, ask pupils, eg 'Welche Farbe hat der Ball?' They must guess/remember the colour. You take that item out of the bag and the pupils either agree, eg 'Ja, er ist grün,' or disagree 'Ach, nein, er ist blau.'

✱ Ask pupils to close their eyes, then hand them each an item that they have previously seen. Without opening their eyes, they say the colour of the item from memory. They then check and correct themselves if necessary.

✱ Sheet 9c provides reading comprehension, tests colours and introduces opinions.

✱ Extend work on countries and flags. An 'Andere Länder' (Different Countries) display could be made. Pupils could choose a country and use books, the Internet etc to find out further information about the country, including the design/colours of its flag.

Further activities

✱ Pupils all stand up holding their coloured item. You or another pupil call out a colour drawn from a bag. All those with an item of that colour sit down. The winner is the person left standing the longest.

✱ Hide coloured objects around the classroom/hall etc. When you say a colour, pupils must find an object of that colour within a time limit (or while you play some music) and return to their places with it, or touch it when the music stops. Those with no coloured object or the incorrect colour are out of the game. Plan the game so that there will only be one or two of the last coloured item to find. Players still in the game at the end are the winners.

✱ Pupils could find out more about other German-speaking countries.

Ich wohne in …

I live in …

In welchem Land wohnst du?
In which country do you live?

Ich heiße Emilio.
Ich wohne in

_____.

Ich heiße Jane.
Ich wohne in

_____.

Ich heiße David.
Ich wohne in

_____.

Irland Schottland
Nordirland
die Niederlande
England Dänemark
Wales Deutschland Polen
Belgien
Frankreich Österreich
Italien
Spanien die Schweiz

Ich heiße Dieter.
Ich wohne in

_____.

Ich heiße Claudette.
Ich wohne in

_____.

Ich heiße Gordon.
Ich wohne in

_____.

Ich heiße Mario.
Ich wohne in

_____.

Ich heiße Jakob.
Ich wohne in

_____.

Ich heiße Heidi.
Ich wohne in

_____.

Ich heiße Bernadette.
Ich wohne in

_____.

Das ist Deutsch!
© *Kathy Williams and Amanda Doyle*

Welche Farben hat die Nationalflagge von ... ?

What colour is the national flag of ... ?

Guten Tag, ich heiße _____.

Ich wohne in _____.

Ich bin _____.

Die Flagge ist _____.

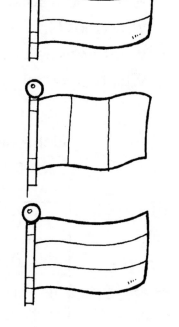

Die österreichische Flagge ist weiß und rot.

Die italienische Flagge ist grün, weiß und rot.

Die spanische Flagge ist rot und gelb.

Die französische Flagge ist blau, weiß und rot.

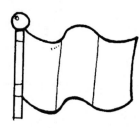

Das ist Deutsch!
www.brilliantpublications.co.uk

Wir reden über Farben

We are talking about colours

Bitte lesen und auf Englisch antworten:

Please read and answer in English:

Michael: Welche Farbe hast du am liebsten, Marc?

Marc: Blau. Ich habe blau am liebsten.

Michael: Und du, Sofie?

Sofie: Äh … rosa und auch gelb.

Michael: Und du, Manfred?

Manfred: Das ist schwer. Ich habe lila gern und auch grün.

Michael: Welche Farbe hast du am liebsten, Bernhard?

Bernhard: Ich? Ich habe gelb gern. Und ich mag grau nicht.

Michael: Ich habe blau gern, aber wie Bernhard habe ich gelb am liebsten.

1. What question is Michael asking all his friends? _____

    _____

2. What does Marc reply? _____

3. What about Sofie? _____

4. Why does Manfred say it is a difficult question? _____

5. What does Bernhard say? _____

6. Which colour(s) are the most popular? _____

Suche die Farbwörter. Du kannst sie anmalen.

Look for the colours. You can colour them in.

rot
grün
orange
weiß
rosa
lila
blau
gelb
schwarz
braun

L	U	W	T	E	G	N	A	R	O
U	A	L	B	B	A	T	S	O	R
B	J	Z	R	A	W	H	C	S	ß
L	B	G	A	ß	E	I	H	A	R
E	Z	R	U	L	I	L	A	L	O
G	R	Ü	N	S	ß	O	Z	E	T

Das ist Deutsch!

Bist du ein Tierfreund?

Learning objectives

Pupils will be able to:

* Name some animals and say if they have one
* Give simple descriptions of animals
* Express opinions
* Understand construction of plurals

Resources needed

* Sheets 10a, 10b, 10c, 10d
* German foods/fruit (optional); sticky labels; animal models/toys.

Activities

* Introduce animal words (pets) with flashcards sheet 10a.

* Place the animal cards face down. A pupil chooses one. Without looking, he/she takes a guess ('Es ist ein/eine …),' checks and class agrees with 'Ja, es ist … ' or corrects with 'Nein, es ist … '. The winner is the first person to guess correctly.

* Sheet 10b is a vocabulary-matching exercise. It uses the question 'Was ist es?' (Note that articles are given ready in the accusative form.)

* Introduce the question 'Magst du Tiere?' and the responses 'Ja, ich mag' or 'Nein, ich mag keine Tiere.' Go round the group asking pupils for responses.

Schlüsselwörter – Key words	
die Tiere	animals
die Haustiere	pets
Was ist es?	What is it?
die Katze	cat
die Maus	mouse
der Hund	dog
die Spinne	spider
das Pferd	horse
das Kaninchen	rabbit
der Fisch	fish
der Vogel	bird
das Meerschweinchen	guinea pig
orange	orange
weiß	white
braun	brown
grau	grey
Magst du … ?	Do you like … ?
Ich mag …	I like …
Ich mag kein(e) …	I don't like …
Ich mag … nicht	I don't like …
Ich habe ...	I have ... (plus accusative)
er ist/sie ist/es ist …	It is … (masculine/feminine/neuter)
klein	small
groß	big
süß	cute/sweet

* Use flashcards (sheet 10a) to focus on creating questions similar to those on sheet 10c. Elicit replies from the group.

* Sheet 10c. Pupils survey a selection of classmates and record their replies in German. The spoken replies must be in full sentences using 'Ja, ich mag … '/ 'Nein, ich mag kein … '.

✻ Practise the question 'Hast du ein Tier?' and the reply 'Ja, ich habe ein Tier. Ich habe einen/ein/eine … '. Pupils could reply with own animals. (You may need a dictionary to look up further words.) Alternatively, pupils could each have an animal flashcard (sheet 10a) and say 'Ich habe einen/ein/eine … '.

✻ Write the names of animals on sticky labels. Stick one on the back of each pupil, without letting them read the labels first. Each pupil must discover what pet he/she has by asking 'Habe ich einen/ein/eine … ?' to another pupil, who replies simply with 'Ja' or 'Nein'. Everyone continues asking, to a different classmate each time, until they have discovered what animal name is on their back.

✻ Sheet 10d. Call out descriptions using colours from Unit 9, plus other adjectives. Pupils listen to each description, and identify the correct animals.

✻ Pupils can be encouraged to describe their own pets and draw them (could be used for display).

Further activities

✻ Pupils mime or make animal noises for their partner to guess, using 'Es ist ein/ eine … '.

✻ Follow up the survey (sheet 10c) by drawing a graph/pie chart to show popularity of animals. 'Das beliebteste Tier ist … '.

✻ Provide a selection of German foods/fruits for pupils to taste (some are named on sheet 10c) or use fruits, drinks etc. Pupils record opinions using 'Ich mag … ' or 'Ich mag … nicht.' The food items named on the sheet are as follows:

Stollen	Bread-like cake, usually eaten during the Christmas season
Sauerkraut	Pickled cabbage
Schwarzwälder Kirschtorte	Black Forest Gateau
Schwarzbrot	Brown bread
Reibekuchen mit Apfelmus	Cake with apple jam

✻ Encourage pupils to use dictionaries to prepare further surveys on other topics.

Haustiere (Karten)

Das ist Deutsch!

Haustiere

Pets

Was ist das?
What is it?

ein Hund   eine Katze   ein Pferd

ein Kaninchen   eine Spinne   ein Meerschweinchen

ein Fisch   eine Maus   ein Vogel

Es ist eine Katze.

Es ist _____.

Es ist _____.

Es ist _____.

Es ist _____.

Es ist_____.

Es ist _____.

Es ist _____.

Es ist _____.

Das ist Deutsch!

Bist du ein Tierfreund?

Are you an animal lover?

Eine Umfrage

A survey

Frage deine Freunde.

Ask your friends.

Schreib 'Ja' oder 'Nein'.

Freund(in) ...	1	2	3	4
Magst du ...				
Hunde?				
Fische?				
Katzen?				
Spinnen?				
Mäuse?				
Vögel?				
Pferde?				

Das beliebteste Tier ist _____

Deutsches Essen

Magst du ...   eg   Ja, ich mag Stollen.

Nein, ich mag keinen Stollen.

Sauerkraut?   _____.

Schwarzwälder Kirschtorte?   _____.

Schwarzbrot?   _____.

Reibekuchen mit Apfelmus?   _____.

Das ist Deutsch!

Es ist klein und orange …

It is small and orange …

Welches Tier ist das? Schreibe die Nummer dazu und male die Tiere an.

Which animal is it? Write the number and colour the animal in.

1) Er ist klein und orange.

2) Es ist groß und grau.

3) Sie ist schwarz und weiß. Sie ist süß.

4) Sie ist klein und schwarz.

5) Er ist klein und blau und grün.

6) Sie ist klein und weiß.

Das ist Deutsch! © Kathy Williams and Amanda Doyle

Meine Familie

Learning objectives

Pupils will be able to:

* Describe who is in their family or who someone is
* Use mein/meine (possessive)
* Use hair and eye colour descriptions for self and others

Resources needed

* Sheets 11a, 11b, 11c, 11d
* Family photographs; dolls; puppets.

Activities

* Introduce 'Das ist meine Familie,' 'Das ist mein Vater' and 'Das ist meine Mutter.'

* Revise 'Ich heiße … '.

* On sheet 11a, ask pupils to draw 'father' and 'mother' faces onto the seaside pictures. Cut the sheets into four. The pupils then pick a card at random and show it to the group, saying either 'Das ist mein Vater' or 'Das ist meine Mutter.' Highlight the possessive, mein/meine (see Grammar Points).

* Introduce the question: 'Hast du Geschwister?' Pupils reply 'Ich habe einen Bruder,' 'Ich habe zwei Schwestern' or 'Ich habe einen Bruder und eine Schwester,' accordingly, or 'Ich habe keine Geschwister' if they are an only child.

* Sheet 11b. In exercise 1, pupils need to draw lines to link the children on the left with their brothers/sisters on the right and write appropriate sentences. This exercise revises numbers one to five (see Unit 5).

* Practise the question: 'Wer ist das?' (possibly with photos/drawings of the child's family). On sheet 11b, exercise 2, pupils look at the pictures (for exercises 1 and 2) and complete the sentences.

Schlüsselwörter – Key words

Das ist/sind	This is/These are
Mein/meine	my (see Grammar Points for correct endings)
meine Mutter	my mother
mein Vater	my father
ein Bruder	a (one) brother
eine Schwester	a sister
Geschwister	siblings
Ich habe …	I have … (plus accusative)
kein/keine	no/none (see Grammar Points for endings)
Wer ist das?	Who is it?
die Haare	hair
die Augen	eyes
braun	brown
rot	red/ginger
blond	blond
schwarz	black
blau	blue
grün	green
Er hat …	He has …
Sie hat …	She has …

✳   Distribute family group cards (sheet 11c), one per pupil. There are 30 cards in total, divided into 10 horizontal family groups of 3. (If you have fewer pupils, divide the cards appropriately. For example, if you have 10 pupils, use 2 x sets of 3 and 2 x sets of 2. For 20 pupils, use 6 x sets of 3 and 1 x set of 2 etc. For sets of 2, white out the names that don't apply.) Pupils circulate around the class, saying 'Guten Tag, ich heiße … ' then, for example, 'Ich habe einen Bruder Paul und eine Schwester Marie.' If the person they are talking to matches the family group by being Paul or Marie, they introduce themselves and then go as a pair in search of their missing third person. When all the family sets are complete, the pupils could introduce themselves.

✳   Using family photographs, pupils explain who is who in the picture using 'Das ist mein Bruder/Das ist meine Schwester' etc, in pairs or to the group.

✳   Introduce the words for hair, eyes etc, plus adjectives for describing their colour.

✳   Pupils describe own hair and eyes using 'Ich habe rote Haare/Ich habe blaue Augen' (see Grammar Points for adjective endings).

✳   Use dolls, puppets etc to reinforce 'Er hat braune Haare' and 'Sie hat grüne Augen' etc (see Grammar Points for adjective endings). Pupils could colour in each of the four hair/eye colours on the four people on sheet 11a. They could then describe to a partner the colours they have given to their characters' hair and eyes. They could colour further pictures with funny hair/ eye colour choices.

✳   Pupils describe their own family members. Sheet 11d provides further reinforcement: pupils draw and describe themselves and a family member (this will involve use of colour adjectives in the plural).

Further activities

✳   Pupils could draw a family picture and write descriptions to match using the language in this unit.

✳   Work in pairs. Pupils study each other's family photographs, then hide them from view. Pupils take it in turns to describe each other's relatives using, eg 'Er hat braune Augen' when prompted by 'mein Bruder'/'meine Schwester'/'mein Vater' etc.

✳   Pupils describe a class member and others guess the person.

✳   'Wer ist das?' (Who is it?) could be the title of a 'baby photo' identity parade, where pupils must work out whom the pictures belong to – other pupils or teachers!

Das ist Deutsch!   © *Kathy Williams and Amanda Doyle*

Das ist mein Vater, das ist meine Mutter

This is my dad, this is my mum

Das ist Deutsch!

Hast du Geschwister?

Do you have any siblings?

Exercise 1

Verbinde die Kinder mit ihrer Familie.
Join the children with their families.

Ich habe einen Bruder und eine Schwester.

_____

_____

_____

_____

_____

Exercise 2

Wer ist das?
Who is it?

1   ?   Das ist mein Bruder.

2   ?   Das ist meine _____.

3   ?   Das ist _____.

4   ?   Das ist _____.

Das ist Deutsch!   © Kathy Williams and Amanda Doyle

Brüder und Schwestern

Brothers and sisters

1 Bruder Paul **Marcel** 1 Schwester Marie	1 Bruder Marcel **Paul** 1 Schwester Marie	1 Bruder Marcel **Marie** 1 Bruder Paul
1 Bruder Michael **Tim** 1 Schwester Lena	1 Bruder Tim **Michael** 1 Schwester Lena	1 Bruder Tim **Lena** 1 Bruder Michael
1 Bruder Jonas **Lukas** 1 Schwester Anna	1 Bruder Lukas **Jonas** 1 Schwester Anna	1 Bruder Lukas **Anna** 1 Bruder Jonas
1 Bruder Moritz **Max** 1 Schwester Leonie	1 Bruder Max **Moritz** 1 Schwester Leonie	1 Bruder Max **Leonie** 1 Bruder Moritz
1 Bruder Tobias **Viktoria** 1 Schwester Sofie	1 Bruder Tobias **Sofie** 1 Schwester Viktoria	1 Schwester Viktoria **Tobias** 1 Schwester Sofie
1 Bruder Alexander **Julia** 1 Schwester Katharina	1 Bruder Alexander **Katharina** 1 Schwester Julia	1 Schwester Julia **Alexander** 1 Schwester Katharina
1 Bruder Manfred **Johanna** 1 Schwester Sabine	1 Bruder Manfred **Sabine** 1 Schwester Johanna	1 Schwester Johanna **Manfred** 1 Schwester Sabine
1 Bruder Hans **Anja** 1 Schwester Ute	1 Bruder Hans **Ute** 1 Schwester Anja	1 Schwester Anja **Hans** 1 Schwester Ute
1 Bruder Dirk **Felix** 1 Bruder David	1 Bruder David **Dirk** 1 Bruder Felix	1 Bruder Felix **David** 1 Bruder Dirk
1 Schwester Heike **Katja** 1 Schwester Ursula	1 Schwester Katja **Heike** 1 Schwester Ursula	1 Schwester Katja **Ursula** 1 Schwester Heike

Das ist Deutsch!

www.brilliantpublications.co.uk

Ich habe braune Augen

I've got brown eyes

Fülle die Einzelheiten aus.

Fill in the details.

Ich bin's.

Ich habe _____ Haare.

Ich habe _____ Augen.

Das ist _____.

Er/sie hat _____ Haare.

Er hat _____ Augen.

Er hat ...
He has ...

Sie hat ...
She has ...

Das ist Deutsch!   © *Kathy Williams and Amanda Doyle*

Bruder Jakob

Brother James

Singe diese Lied.
Sing this song.

Bruder Jakob, Bruder Jakob,
Schläfst du noch? Schläfst du noch?
Hörst du nicht die Glocken?
Hörst du nicht die Glocken?

Ding, dang, dong.
Ding, dang, dong.

   www.brilliantpublications.co.uk

Die Ferien

Learning objectives

Pupils will be able to:

* Say where they are going using 'Ich fahre … '
* Use some destinations using 'ans'/'aufs'/'in'/'nach'
* Talk about modes of transport using 'mit dem'/'zu'
* Ask where someone is going

Resources needed

* Sheets 12a, 12b, 12c, 12d
* Map; ribbon/string; magazine travel pictures; travel brochures.

Activities

* Introduce the question 'Wohin fährst du?' and three holiday areas (beach/country/mountains) using 'Ich fahre … '. Use flashcards (sheet 12a) to aid comprehension. Pupils choose a destination they would prefer using 'Ich fahre … '.

* Introduce the use of 'Ich fahre nach' + town.

* Explain that when we are going to a country, we use 'Ich fahre nach' + country. When combining a place and a country, however (eg 'Ich fahre aufs Land in Frankreich'), the 'nach' changes to 'in'. Ask pupils to suggest their own destinations using 'Ich fahre ans Meer … etc' and a country name (see Unit 9 for country names).

* Sheet 12b reinforces the use of 'Ich fahre ans/aufs/in/nach … '.

* Introduce modes of transport using the flashcards on sheet 12c.

* Use flashcards (sheet 12c). Hold them up and ask the pupils to select one form of transport. Turn the cards over, then ask several pupils to pick one card each, without looking at the pictures. The one who has chosen the form of transport that the class decided on earlier is the one who is 'going

Schlüsselwörter – Key words

Wohin fährst du?/ Wohin fahren Sie?	Where are you going?
Ich fahre …	I am going …
ans Meer	to the seaside
aufs Land	to the countryside
in die Berge	to the mountains
nach/in Deutschland	to/in Germany
nach/in Schottland	to/in Scotland
nach/in Irland	to/in Ireland
nach/in London	to/in London
nach/in Cardiff	to/in Cardiff
macht Ferien	on holiday
mit dem Bus (m)	by bus
mit dem Schiff (n)	by boat
mit dem Fahrrad (n)	by bicycle
mit dem Auto (n)	by car
mit dem Flugzeug (n)	by plane
mit dem Zug (m)	by train
zu Fuß (m)	on foot
zu Pferd (n)	on horseback
Gute Fahrt!	Safe journey!

Das ist Deutsch! © Kathy Williams and Amanda Doyle

on holiday'. He/she says, eg 'Ich fahre nach Berlin,' and adds on the form of transport, eg 'Ich fahre mit dem Flugzeug nach Berlin.' Everyone else says 'Gute Fahrt!' and the game continues until everyone 'macht Ferien'.

✳ Sheet 12d. Give each pupil a copy of sheet 12d. They play in pairs. Each pupil hides their grid from their partner and draws the seven forms of transport in his/her grid, using the words, too, if wished. Player 1 reads out a numbered grid reference in German. If their partner has a picture in that square, he/she says 'Ja'. Player 1 then guesses the transport word, eg 'ein Pferd' (all words take 'ein', except for 'Fuß', which becomes 'Füße' because there are two!). If they are right the picture is crossed off and Player 1 continues. If wrong, Player 2 has a turn and Player 1 must wait his/her turn to guess another form of transport for that box. The winner is the player who guesses all his/her opponent's positions and transport correctly.

✳ Pupils use question 'Wohin fährst du?' to ask each other where they are going 'in den Ferien' for the next approaching holiday period. Pupils can try to explain as far as possible where, how and when they are going. (For dates, refer to Unit 8.) Explain to the pupils that sentence order usually follows the rule Time/Manner/Place.

✳ Use cut-up travel brochures or magazine pictures for pupils to invent future travel plans/itineraries.

Further activities

✳ Using a map, pupils could mark places to be visited in the holidays and connect these to 'home' with a ribbon, string or drawn line. They could write short descriptions of how their places are to be reached, eg 'Ich fliege mit dem Flugzeug nach Spanien.' Pupils could make small transport symbols, labelled in German, to attach to the connecting line.

✳ A transport frieze could be made around the room.

In den Ferien

On holiday

Das ist Deutsch!

© Kathy Williams and Amanda Doyle

Wohin fährst du in den Ferien?

Where are you going on holiday?

Exercise 1

Verbinde die Tiere mit ihrem Ferienort:

Match the animals with their holiday destinations:

aufs Land   ans Meer   in die Berge

Exercise 2

Ich fahre ...

... nach Berlin

... in Deutschland

... nach Rom

... in Italien

Wohin fahren

Dieter und Gianni?

Dieter: Ich fahre _____

Gianni: Ich fahre _____

Das ist Deutsch!

www.brilliantpublications.co.uk

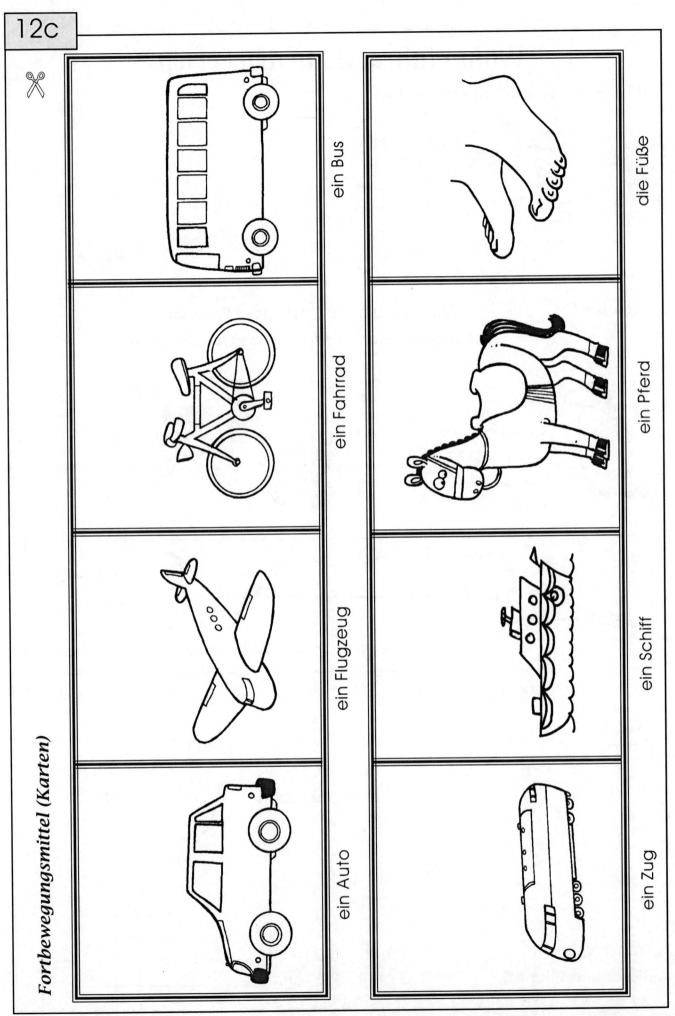

Fortbewegungsmittel (Karten)

ein Bus

die Füße

ein Fahrrad

ein Pferd

ein Flugzeug

ein Schiff

ein Auto

ein Zug

Das ist Deutsch!

© Kathy Williams and Amanda Doyle

Das Reise-Spiel

The transport game

ein Fahrrad 4

ein Auto 3

ein Bus 2

ein Flugzeug 1

	A	B	C

Zeichne sieben Fortbewegungsmittel in die Tabelle ein, wo du willst. Es bleiben fünf Plätze leer.

Draw seven modes of transport in the grid, wherever you want. There will be five empty boxes.

die Füße

ein Schiff

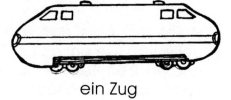

ein Zug

Das ist Deutsch!
www.brilliantpublications.co.uk

Mein Tag

Learning objectives

Pupils will be able to:

* Describe some activities using common verbs.
* Say what the time is, on the hour
* Talk about school subjects they like/don't like
* Describe the school day

Resources needed

* Sheets 13a, 13b, 13c, 13d, 13e
* Pupils' school timetable; clock faces.

Activities

* Weather expressions (fine, awful, snowing, raining) revised from Unit 4.

* Introduce 'Wenn es regnet, bleibe ich zu Hause' etc to go with the pictures in 13a. Pupils then pick a picture to go with each weather expression/ situation the teacher says. Highlight 'wenn'. In English, discuss what activities you could do 'Wenn es schrecklich ist/es sonnig ist' etc (German verbs are introduced in the next activity).

* Introduce the 'activity phrases' listed in the Schlüsselwörter, and additional ones suggested by the children. Encourage pupils to complete the weather sentences with an appropriate activity phrase in German.

* Sheet 13b. Pupils match weather and activity choices.

* Sheet 13c shows 'daily routine' activities. Give each pupil a strip and ask them to cut it up and mix up the pieces. The teacher (or

Schlüsselwörter – Key words

wann?	when?
wenn?	if/when?
die Freizeit	free time
ich spiele	I play
ich sehe fern	I watch television
ich bleibe	I stay
ich esse	I eat
ich rede	I talk
ich gehe	I go/walk
ich arbeite	I work
ich komme nach Hause	I arrive home
ich höre	I listen
es ist … Uhr	it is … o'clock
um … Uhr	at … o'clock
am Mittag	at midday
um Mitternacht	at midnight
mein Stunden-plan (m)	my timetable
Mathe (f)	maths
Naturwissen-schaft (f)	science
Sport (m)	sport
Deutsch (n)	German
Kunst (f)	art
Englisch (n)	English
Geisteswissen-schaften (pl)	humanities
Musik (f)	music
Informatik (f)	ICT
toll	great
interessant	interesting
langweilig	boring
zu schwer	too difficult
wunderbar	wonderful

Das ist Deutsch!   © Kathy Williams and Amanda Doyle

the children, if able) then calls out in German the order in which the activities could be done. Highlight the use of 'Ich' + verb.

✳   Sheet 13d: pupils stick pictures (from sheet 13c) in the correct order and fill in the verbs. Highlight how all the verbs end in 'e'.

✳   Look at sheet 13d. Agree with the pupils when each of the activities might take place (to the nearest hour). Display clock faces for the agreed times in a prominent position. Call out times to introduce 'Es ist … Uhr' and 'Es ist Mittag.' Mime the activities. Pupils have to give an appropriate time. For example, if you mime eating breakfast, they might say 'Es ist sieben Uhr.'

✳   Repeat the above activity, but this time give a time, eg 'Es ist neun Uhr.' The pupils might respond 'Ich gehe zur Schule.' They could practise this in pairs as well.

✳   Sheet 13d, exercise 2. Pupils match the times on the clocks with the phrases, writing the corresponding number in the boxes beneath the clocks.

✳   Introduce school subjects. Using sheet 13e, pupils listen to the teacher describing the lessons on each day and try to identify which day is being referred to. Pupils could pretend to be Markus and make up phrases about the school day based on his timetable, eg 'Um … Uhr, habe ich' + subject.

✳   Pupils can create their own sentences and phrases using their own school timetable.

✳   Introduce adjectives to describe school subjects. Pupils express opinions about school subjects and fill in sheet 13e, exercise 2.

Further activities

✳   Practise times by pinning clock faces round the room showing different times. Pupils point to or collect the correct clock to show understanding. Pupils could work in pairs to test each other.

✳   Pupils could find out more about German school customs and the school day in Germany. They could compare their subject areas with those from Germany. You could discuss how English would be the equivalent 'foreign language' for German children.

✳   Pupils could draw up a bar chart of preferred/least-liked subjects labelled in German.

Das Wetter (Karten)

Das ist Deutsch!

© Kathy Williams and Amanda Doyle

Meine Freizeit

My free time

Verbinde die Tätigkeit mit dem Wetter:

Join the activity with the weather:

Wenn es schön ist …

spiele ich im Garten.

Wenn es schneit …

sehe ich fern.

Wenn es schrecklich ist …

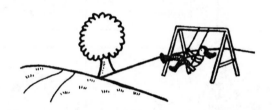

spiele ich im Park.

Wenn es regnet …

bleibe ich zu Hause.

Wenn es heiß ist …

spiele ich im Garten.

Das ist Deutsch!

www.brilliantpublications.co.uk

Die tägliche Routine (Karten)

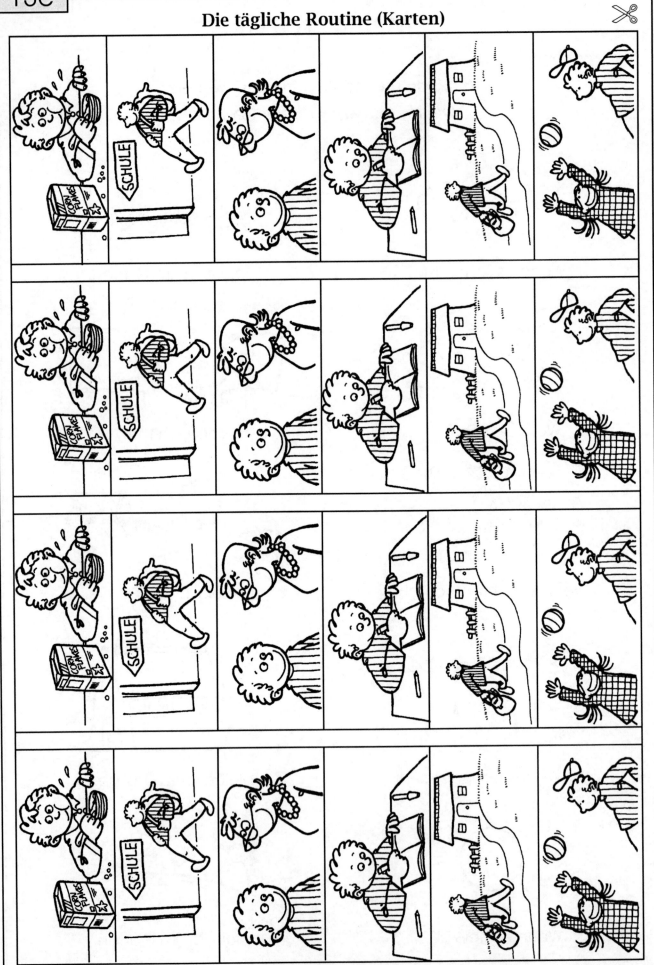

Das ist Deutsch!

Ein Tag in der Schule

A day at school

Fülle die Lücken aus:
Fill in the blanks:

Exercise 1

Ich _____ mein Frühstück.

Ich _____ zur Schule.

Ich _____ mit der Lehrerin.

Ich _____ im Klassenzimmer.

Ich _____ nach Hause.

Ich _____ mit meinen Freunden.

esse

spiele

komme

rede

gehe

arbeite

Exercise 2 **Trage die richtigen Zahlen ein:**

Write in the correct number:

1. Es ist zehn Uhr.
2. Es ist sieben Uhr.
3. Es ist vier Uhr.
4. Es ist neun Uhr.

Das ist Deutsch!

Mein Stundenplan

My timetable

Exercise 1 **Höre zu und sage welcher Tag es ist.**

Listen and decide which day it is.

Hier ist mein Stundenplan.

Markus

	9		10		11	12	1–2	4
Montag	Mathe				Naturwissenschaft		Sport	
Dienstag	Englisch				Deutsch		Naturwissen-schaft	
Mittwoch	Kunst		Musik		Deutsch	Geisteswissen-schaft	Sport	
Donnerstag	Musik		Mathe		Geisteswissen-schaft	Naturwissen-schaft	Informatik	
Freitag	Englisch				Kunst	Sport	Mathe	

Exercise 2 **Beantworte die Fragen.**

Answer the questions.

 Ich mag Kunst. Sie ist toll.
Und du? _____

 Ich mag Mathe. Sie ist interessant.
Und du? _____

Ich mag Musik. Sie ist wunderbar.
Und du? _____

 Ich mag Sport nicht. Er ist langweilig.
Und du? _____

 Ich mag Englisch nicht. Es ist zu schwer.
Und du? _____

Das ist Deutsch!

Das Essen

Learning objectives

Pupils will be able to:

* Talk about food for a picnic
* Use words for 'some'
* Say 'I would like … ', 'please' and 'thank you'.
* Use numbers up to 100

Resources needed

* Sheets 14a, 14b, 14c, 14d, 14e
* Real food items (bread, butter, ham, cheese, crisps etc); tablecloths; notepads for 'waiters'; sticky labels; variety of goods 'for sale'.

Activities

* Talk about what foods you might take on a picnic. Using the flashcards on sheet 14a (or the real thing), introduce the phrase 'Möchtes du etwas?' Pupils choose from what is on offer. Pupils reply using 'ja/nein'. Introduce 'Ich möchte ein/eine/ einen' at the same time. Pupils could use this phrase to ask for items. Highlight 'etwas/ein/eine/ einen', and when each is used. If you are using real food, you could have 'ein Picknick' at this stage.

* Sheet 14b reinforces choices – pupils draw chosen foods (you could limit it to five or six), then explain what they would like for a picnic to a partner/to the group. (Revise 'Ich mag … ' from Units 10 and 13.)

* Sheet 14a can also be used to play a game. Photocopy and cut up enough sheets so that

Schlüsselwörter – Key words

ich möchte	I would like
Möchtes du etwas … ?	Would you like some … ?
Brot (n)	bread
Butter (f)	butter
Käse (m)	cheese
Schinken (m)	ham
Schokolade (f)	chocolate
Cola (f)	Coke
Pommes Frites (n pl)	chips
Äpfel (m pl)	apples
Kartoffelchips (m pl)	crisps
Kuchen (m)	cake
ein Tee (m)	a tea
ein Kaffee (m)	a coffee
ein Mineral- wasser (n)	a mineral water
ein Saft (m)	a fruit juice
eine Zitronen- limonade (f)	a lemonade (traditional)
ein Hot Dog (m)	a hot dog
eine Pizza (f)	a pizza
ein Hörnchen (n)	a croissant
ein Sandwich (n)	a sandwich
ein Schinken- sandwich	a ham sandwich
ein Käsesandwich	a cheese sandwich
Haben Sie eine Wahl getroffen?	Have you made your choice?
hier	here (you are)
danke	thank you
bitte	please
Das macht 50 Euros	That comes to 50 Euros

each pupil has three cards. Pupils play in groups of six. The aim is for each pupil to try to collect all the food from the other players in his/her group. Player 1 starts by asking anyone else for a card by saying, eg 'Ich möchte etwas Brot' to collect a food item he/she does not have. If that person has the requested card, he/she hands it over, saying 'Hier, bitte.' Player 1 continues until he/she makes a mistake by asking for a card that someone does not have. It is then that player's turn to say 'Ich möchte etwas/ein/ eine/einen ... ' to another player. He may, of course, ask for the card that Player 1 has just acquired. This game tests memory as well as vocabulary!

✳ Introduce more food vocabulary using sheet 14c. Fill in vocabulary. Highlight what might be asked in a café eg 'Haben Sie eine Wahl getroffen?' and the use of 'ein Tee/Cola' etc.

✳ Pupils could design their own café menus. You could talk about different German eating places and 'Kaffee und Kuchen'. Dictionaries could be used to expand the dishes/drinks on offer.

✳ Build up a café dialogue using phrases already learned. Pupils can fill in the gaps on sheet 14d. Highlight prices in the menu, please and thank you.

✳ Using pupils' menus and tables laid out café-style, pupils role-play a café scene. You could record or video for the class or others. Encourage use of further conversation, if possible, particularly stating opinions about the food (Units 9, 10 and 13).

✳ Practise numbers up to 100. Sheet 14e helps to reinforce larger numbers.

Further activities

✳ Pupils could design a poster to advertise their café. They could use ICT facilities to print a poster/flyer.

✳ Pupils could research German regional dishes and products.

✳ Numbers practice can come from a food-price guessing game. Present pupils with a variety of goods in a wide price range. Stick a label on the base of each with a price in Euros from 1–100. Look up the exchange rate in a newspaper or on teletext. Pupils guess (in teams) what the prices could be in British sterling. The team with the closest amount wins a point, and the most correct/close answers wins the game.

Ein Picknick

For a picnic

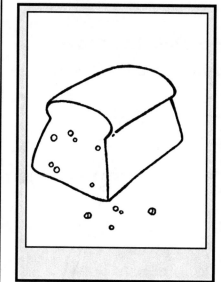
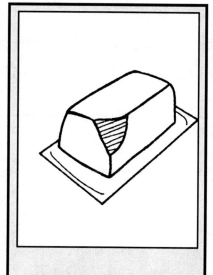
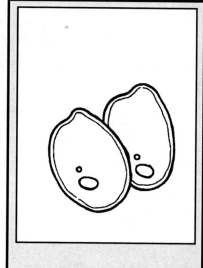

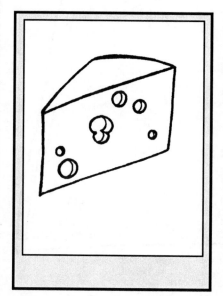

Kartoffelchips

Das ist Deutsch!

www.brilliantpublications.co.uk

Machen wir uns ein Picknick?

Shall we have a picnic?

Wähle das Essen für das Picknick aus. Zeichne es auf die Tischdecke.

Choose what you would like for a picnic. Draw them on the tablecloth.

Das ist Deutsch!

Im Café

At the café

Ich möchte ...   **und ...**
I would like ...   *and ...*

_____

_____

_____

_____

_____

_____

_____

_____

_____

_____

_____

_____

ein Tee   eine Cola

eine Zitronenlimonade

ein Mineralwasser

einen Kaffee mit Milch

ein Saft

ein Hörnchen

ein Käsesandwich

eine Pizza   Pommes Frites

ein Schinkensandwich

ein Hot Dog

Haben Sie eine Wahl getroffen?

Have you made a choice?

Lies die Speisekarte.

Read the menu.

ein Kaffee
ein Tee €4.00
eine Cola €3.60
ein Saft €4.00
ein Mineralwasser €3.80
€1.50

Speisekarte
ein Hot Dog €4.75
eine Pizza €4.00
ein Schinkensandwich €5.10
ein Käsesandwich €4.90

Lies das Gespräch durch. Fülle die Lücken aus:

Read the conversation. Fill in the spaces:

Max: Möchtes du eine Cola, Lena?

Lena: Ja, ich möchte eine Cola, bitte.

Max: Ich möchte _____ _____.

Lena: Ich möchte ein Sandwich und _____ _____

der Ober: Guten Tag. Haben Sie eine Wahl getroffen?

Max: Ja. Ich möchte _____ _____, bitte.

Lena: Und ich möchte _____ _____, Pommes

              Frites und eine Cola, bitte.

der Ober: Hier, bitte, _____ _____ , _____ _____ ,

              Pommes Frites und _____. Das macht _____ Euros.

Max: Hier. Vielen Dank.

Das ist Deutsch!

Die Zahlen 20+

Numbers 20+

20 – zwanzig

30 – dreißig

40 – vierzig   50 – fünfzig

60 – sechzig

70 – siebzig

80 – achtzig

90 – neunzig

100 – ein hundert

21	– einundzwanzig	23	– dreiundzwanzig
31	– ____unddreißig	35	– fünfund_____
41	– einund_____	47	– _____vierzig
51	– _____	68	– _____

101 – (ein)hundert-eins   106 – (ein)hundert-sechs

110 – (ein)hundert-zehn   182 – (ein)hundert-zweiundachtzig

200 – zweihundert   202 – zweihundert-zwei

1 000 – (ein)tausend

150 – (ein)hundert-_____   173 – _____ -

2 000 – zweitausend   dreiund _____

2 009 – _____ - _____   3 028 – _____ -

_____

Das ist Deutsch!   81

www.brilliantpublications.co.uk

Ich bin sportlich

Learning objectives

Pupils will be able to:

* Talk about parts of the body
* Name some common sports
* Express opinions about sports

Resources needed

* Sheets 15a, 15b, 15c, 15d, 15e
* Dice.

Activities

* Sing 'Head, shoulders, knees and toes' in German and encourage pupils to join in the actions. The words are on sheet 15a.

* Ask pupils to give examples of body parts that they remember from the song.

* Sheet 15b is a vocabulary-matching exercise for parts of the body. You can call out the answers, or the pupils can check their work in pairs or groups.

Schlüsselwörter – Key words

der Kopf	the head
das Bein	the leg
der Mund	the mouth
die Hand	the hand
der Fuß	the foot
das Knie	the knee
der Arm	the arm
die Nase	the nose
der Magen	the stomach
die Haare (pl)	the hair
das Auge	the eye
die Augen	the eyes
die Ohren	the ears
die Schulter	the shoulder
ich spiele …	I play … (+ sport)
ich mache …	I do … (+ sport)
ich gehe …	I go … (+ sport)

* Divide the class into groups of three or four, giving each pupil a person from sheet 15c, together with chopped up pieces of the same character. Each piece is numbered. Player 1 throws the dice and picks up one part of his person with that number on, stating the body part(s) pictured. The winner is the first player to complete his/her figure.

* Call out the parts of the body using 'Zeige mir … '. Pupils respond by touching the body part called. They could then practise the same commands and responses in pairs.

* Sheet 15d extends the exercise theme by introducing various sports. Pupils listen to the teacher and identify which sport is being referred to. They write the corresponding letters in the gaps. You could ask them to give their responses to the group using the alphabet in German.

* Remind pupils of 'Ich mag … ' and 'Ich mag … nicht' (Unit 10). Introduce 'Ich mache … ' and 'Ich gehe … ', and recall 'Ich spiele … ' (Unit 13).

Das ist Deutsch! © Kathy Williams and Amanda Doyle

✳   Ask pupils the question 'Welcher Sport machst du?' Note replies from three or more pupils, writing their names in the sport boxes at the bottom of sheet 15d. Pupils should use 'Ich spiele'/'Ich mache'/'Ich gehe' to reply.

✳   Pupils could fill in the pie-chart on sheet 15e to show the popularity of different sports. You could talk about sports that are popular in Germany and about any German sports stars whom pupils have seen or heard of: Boris Becker (Tennis), Michael Schumacher (F1), Jürgen Klinsmann (Football).

✳   Pupils could use dictionaries to compile an extended list of sports in German.

Further activities

✳   To practise body parts, pupils draw a head and neck on the top third of a piece of paper. They fold the paper backwards so that only the neck is showing and pass the paper to someone else. The next person draws the torso and the start of the legs, folds the paper back and hands it to someone else to draw the legs and feet. This is then passed to a fourth person who opens out the page to reveal a full body. They then name the resulting body parts to the group, pointing them out as they do so.

✳   Pupils could mime sporting actions to each other to identify the sport.

✳   Whisper game: pupils close their eyes and touch the part of their body that you or another pupil whispers to them. Players are out if they are touching the wrong part when they open their eyes.

✳   Mini 'exercise routines'. This game practises numbers as well as body parts. Compile a list of 'exercises', eg 'Berühre die Nase zwanzig mal' (touch your nose 20 times), 'Berühre die Ohren mit der Schulter zwölf mal' (touch your ear with your shoulder 12 times). Each exercise is then performed in pairs, with the pupils counting out in German as they do them. Their partners could time them.

Kopf, Schultern ...

Head, shoulders ...

Singe dieses Lied.
Sing this song.

Kopf, Schultern, Knie und Fuß,
Knie und Fuß.
Kopf, Schultern, Knie und Fuß,
Knie und Fuß.

Augen, Ohren, Mund und Nase.
Kopf, Schultern, Knie und Fuß,
Knie und Fuß.

Das ist Deutsch!

Der Kőrper

The body

Fülle die Lücken aus.

Fill in the blanks.

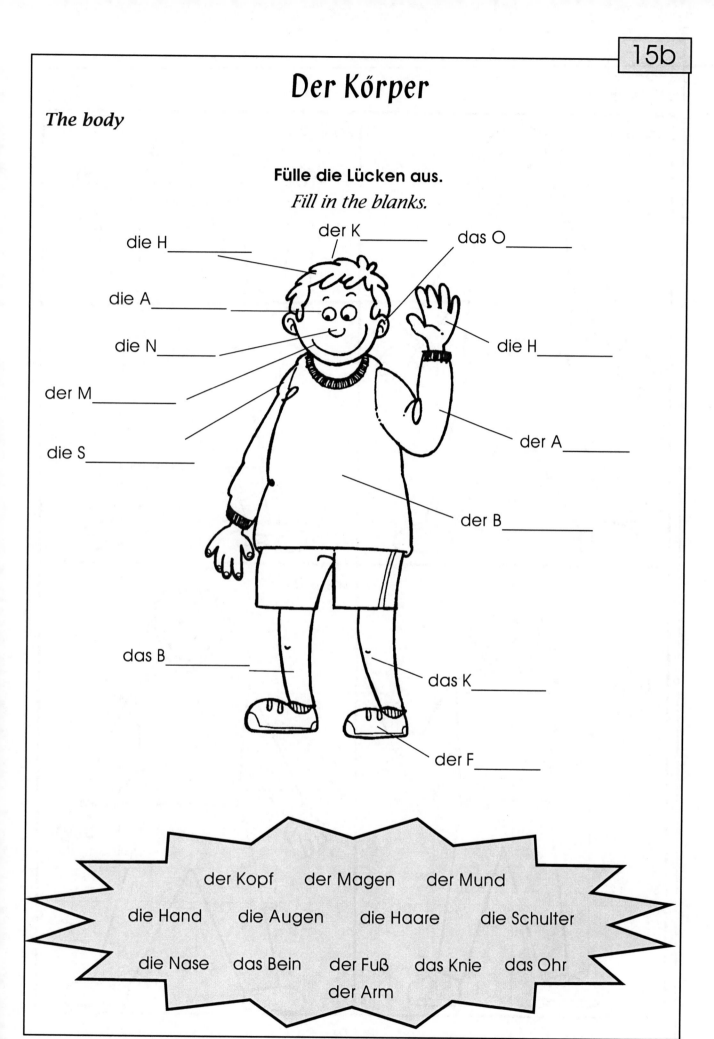

der K_____

das O_____

die H_____

die A_____

die N_____

der M_____

die S_____

die H_____

der A_____

der B_____

das B_____

das K_____

der F_____

der Kopf   der Magen   der Mund

die Hand   die Augen   die Haare   die Schulter

die Nase   das Bein   der Fuß   das Knie   das Ohr

der Arm

Das ist Deutsch!

www.brilliantpublications.co.uk

Die Karten

Karte A

Karte B

Karte C

Karte D

Das ist Deutsch!

Ich turne

I do gymnastics

Was für Sport treibst du?
What sports do you do?

Schreibe die Buchstaben zur richtigen Sportart:
Write the letter next to its sport:

_____	**A** das Fußball
_____	**B** das Rugby
D _____	**C** die Leichtathletik
_____	**D** das Basketball
_____	**E** das Turnen
_____	**F** das Radfahren
_____	**G** das Schwimmen
_____	**H** das Tennis

Was für Sport treibst du? Eine Umfrage
What sports do you do? A survey

Ich spiele	Fußball	Rugby	Basketball	Tennis
Ich gehe	radfahren	schwimmen		tanzen
Ich mache	Leichtathletik		Turnen	

Das ist Deutsch!

www.brilliantpublications.co.uk

Ein Kreisdiagramm der Sportarten

A sports pie-chart

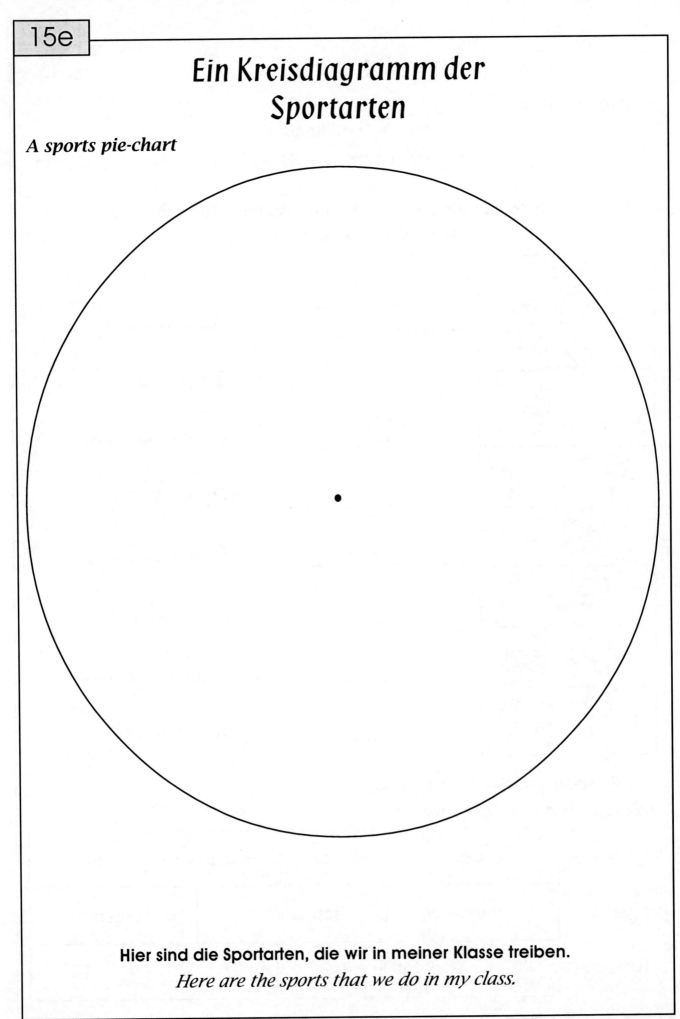

Hier sind die Sportarten, die wir in meiner Klasse treiben.

Here are the sports that we do in my class.

Das ist Deutsch!

© Kathy Williams and Amanda Doyle

Kleidung

Learning objectives

Pupils will be able to:

* Name some common items of clothing
* Say what they wear for different occasions
* Describe their clothes

Resources needed

* Sheets 16a, 16b, 16c
* TV recordings of people; real clothing items; large bag; clothes catalogues/magazine pictures.

Activities

* Introduce the names of items of clothing. Pupils could refer either to sheet 16a (ideally enlarged) or to real items of clothing. The clothes are pictured on the sheet as if they are in a shop window (with the words removed).

* Use real items of clothing or point to an item on the sheet. Suggest to one class member that he/she can take it, eg 'Der Rock?' Pupils could accept, or refuse and make another choice.

Schlüsselwörter – Key words

die Hose	trousers
die Jeans	jeans
das T-shirt	T-shirt
die Shorts	shorts
der Hut	hat
die Krawatte	tie
der Rock	skirt
das Kleid	dress
der Mantel	coat
die Schuluniform	school uniform
die Socken	socks
die Schuhe	shoes
die Turnschuhe	trainers
lang	long
kurz	short
groß	big
klein	small
ich trage	I wear/I am wearing
eine Party	a party

* Using a large bag containing clothes, reveal and name one item at a time. Replace them in the bag and ask pupils if they can remember what items were taken out of the bag and name the clothes in German.

* Pupils match the words from the bottom of sheet 16a with the items pictured. They could cut out the labels and stick them on the picture.

* Pupils could colour in their clothes sheets, then use the sheets as a class exercise to revise colours (from Units 9 and 10), as individuals say which colours they have chosen for their clothing.

* Extend discussion of adjectives to include 'groß' or 'klein' (from Unit 10), and 'lang' or 'kurz'. Pupils could practise using the adjectives by talking about the items on sheet 16a to a partner.

* See Grammar Points on adjectival endings.

✳ Photocopy sheet 16b onto card and cut out the dominoes. Pupils play the game in threes or fours. Player 1 places a double domino on the table. Player 2 must add the opposite to one already down, so if a double noun is on the table, then an adjective should be placed next to one end of the domino. If a player cannot go, the turn passes on to the next player. If no one can take a turn, the next player puts a new double domino card down and the game continues. The winner is the first player to get rid of all his/her dominoes or to have the fewest dominoes left when a maximum of two fresh starts have been made. The sequence of words along the chain should always be matching nouns and adjectives: this practises recognition of 'blauer' as a masculine adjective, 'grüne' as a feminine adjective, 'rotes' as neuter and 'gelben' as plural. Note that this game uses the nominative case.

✳ Pupils could cut out catalogue pictures, and describe what they like about their choice of outfit, eg 'Ich mag die schwarze Hose und das rote T-shirt.' See Grammar Points for guidance.

✳ Introduce 'Ich trage'. Pupils use cut-out pictures or do drawings to illustrate four different types of outfit. They describe to the group what they have chosen – the clothes could be used for a fashion display. Sheet 16c provides a useful visual prompt.

Further activities

✳ Use a recording of a TV show (any show where people are easily seen and clothes can be identified). Show the recording with sound; afterwards ask the pupils to name the items of clothing that they saw people wearing. If you do not prepare the pupils for the clothing questions, this becomes a more challenging 'observation' exercise.

✳ The above activity can be extended to describing the colour and size of clothing, and hair/eye colour (Unit 11). You could arrange for someone to come into the class briefly on some pretext – then afterwards ask pupils to say what he/she was wearing, what he/she looked like and so on.

✳ Pupils could play 'I Spy' in pairs with sheet 16a, revising letters of the alphabet.

✳ Pupils could plan their own 'fashion show'. They could video it and overlay a commentary describing the clothes in German.

Kleidung

Clothes

die Hose	die Jeans	das T-shirt	die Shorts
der Hut	die Krawatte	der Rock	das Kleid
der Mantel	die Socken	die Schuhe	die Turnschuhe

✂ **Schneide die Etiketten aus und klebe Sie an die richtigen Stellen.**

Cut out and stick the labels in place.

Das ist Deutsch!

www.brilliantpublications.co.uk

Dominos

ein blauer	ein blauer	Rock	Rock	eine grüne	eine grüne
Socken	Socken	ein rotes	ein rotes	Hose	Hose
die gelben	Rock	eine grüne	Hose	die gelben	Socken
Kleid	ein rotes	Socken	ein blauer	ein blauer	eine grüne
die gelben	Hose	die gelben	Socken	die gelben	Hose
eine grüne	eine grüne	Kleid	ein rotes	Kleid	Hose
ein blauer	ein blauer	Kleid	die gelben	Hose	ein rotes
Rock	ein rotes	Socken	Hose	eine grüne	Rock
die gelben	Kleid	die gelben	Socken	Kleid	Socken
Rock	eine grüne	Rock	ein rotes	Kleid	ein blauer

Das ist Deutsch!

Ich trage ...

I wear ...

In der Schule trage ich ...

In school I wear ...

In den Ferien trage ich ...

During the holidays I wear ...

Als Sportkleidung trage ich ...

As sportswear I wear ...

Auf einer Party trage ich ...

To a party I wear ...

Das ist Deutsch!

www.brilliantpublications.co.uk

In meiner Stadt

Learning objectives

Pupils will be able to:

* Name common town places/buildings
* Say where places are (left, right, here, there)
* Describe the location of their home town
* Use points of the compass

Resources needed

* Sheets 17a, 17b, 17c
* Town plans; tourist brochures; model buildings (children's wooden toys, for example); names of buildings on large signs.

Activities

* Describe the imaginary town of Gutstadt using the map on sheet 17c.

* Use town plans and tourist brochures of different places, eg London, Berlin, Oxford. Alternatively, list buildings in your home town. Pupils suggest German names for landmarks or buildings. Go through resulting list as a group.

* Pupils could play buildings snap in pairs. Photocopy sheet 17a onto card and cut out the cards. Each player gets 12. They each put down a card at the same time. Pupils say the German word when the pictures on the two cards match. The first to say the word collects the cards. The winner is the first player to collect all the cards.

* Sheet 17b reinforces some vocabulary. Pupils have to solve the anagrams to make building words. You could give them more words to muddle for friends to unravel.

* Introduce the use of 'links' and 'rechts' when giving directions, eg 'links abbiegen'.

Schlüsselwörter – Key words

das Denkmal	monument
das Hotel	hotel
das Museum	museum
das Postamt	post office
das Schwimmbad	swimming pool
der Bahnhof	station (bus/train)
der Parkplatz	car park
der Supermarkt	supermarket
die Bank	bank
die Kirche	church
die Polizeiwache	police station
die Schule	school
links	on the left
rechts	on the right
hier	here
dort	there
da drüben	over there
Wo ist … ?	Where is … ?
im Norden	in the north
im Süden	in the south
im Osten	in the east
im Westen	in the west

Das ist Deutsch!   © Kathy Williams and Amanda Doyle

✸ Using model buildings, make a series of connecting streets, or draw a plan on the board. Pupils take turns to give a series of directions to get from one given point to another. The rest of the group follow the directions and say which building they have reached. The pupil who gave directions confirms or corrects.

✸ Blindfold one pupil and stand him/her in a set place, eg by the door. Another pupil, or group of pupils, gives him/her directions to arrive at a given spot. The blindfolded pupil must obey the instructions correctly. (Further language such as 'geh weiter' (carry on) and 'halt' (stop) may be needed.)

✸ Introduce 'hier', 'dort' and 'da drüben', and practise using them with the question 'Wo ist … ?'

✸ Stick large signs with building names from sheet 17a round the room. Ask, eg 'Wo ist das Postamt?' Pupils point and say, eg 'Dort, links'. Pupils walk around and 'meet' each other as if in the town square. They ask each other where places are and give an appropriate reply.

✸ Using sheet 17c, describe where Berlin is in Germany and the buildings there. Look up famous landmarks on the Internet: Where can the Brandenburg Gate and the Zoological Gardens be found?; Which museums can be found in the Mitte area of Berlin? Talk about the Berlin Wall and how it divided east and west.

✸ Describe Gutstadt again using the map. Highlight 'im Norden/Süden/Osten/Westen'. Pupils can try to identify which buildings are on the Gutstadt plan and name them (sheet 17c).

✸ In groups, pupils could put together a list of places/facilities in their home town, and design a brochure to advertise it. This could be produced on computer or designed to be duplicated on a (colour) photocopier.

Further activities

✸ Pupils could test each other by miming actions connected with a particular building/place. Their partner must guess the place in German.

✸ Pupils could draw town plans in groups of three or four using building words and suggesting 'hier?'/'dort?' when deciding where things should go, eg a hotel next to the main road or a church in the middle of the town.

✸ Pupils could research further information about Berlin or other major towns in Germany.

Schnippschnapp

Das ist Deutsch!

Was ist das?

What is this?

The following are all anagrams. Unscramble and fill in the blanks.

Hier ist:

Here is:

die ceiKhr   = die   **Kirche**

der tupSmerrka   = der   _____

das emMuus   = das   _____

der nohhafB   = der   _____

das tHole   = das   _____

das
dcabwiShmm   = das   _____

Das ist Deutsch!

www.brilliantpublications.co.uk

In Berlin

In Berlin

Stadtplan Berlin

Norden

Westen ⊕ Osten

Süden

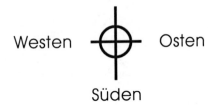

Stadtplan Gutstadt (eine Phantasiestadt)

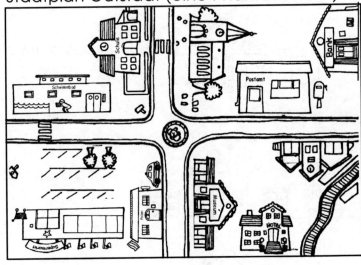

Wo ist?   ... die Bank?
Where is?   ... das Postamt?
                     ... der Supermarkt?

das Denkmal   die Kirche   die Polizeiwache

das Postamt   das Hotel   das Museum

der Bahnhof   der Parkplatz   das Schwimmbad

der Supermarkt   die Schule   die Bank

www.brilliantpublications.co.uk

Das ist Deutsch!   © Kathy Williams and Amanda Doyle

Personalien

Learning objectives

Pupils will be able to:

✱ Give a detailed description of themselves drawing on material from several units

✱ Listen closely and understand longer descriptions of other people

Resources needed

✱ Sheet 18a

✱ Pictures/photographs of famous people; video clips of well-known cartoon or TV characters.

> *Schlüsselwörter – Key words*
>
> Personal descriptions from Units 1, 6, 8, 9, 11 and 17.
>
> Interests and activities from Units 10, 12, 13 and 15.
>
> Opinions from Units 10 and 14.
>
> There are many additional links with other units.

Activities

✱ Display pictures/photographs of well-known people on a board. Describe a number of details about one of them using 'Ich ... ', eg 'Ich habe graue Haare. Ich habe eine Schwester und zwei Brüder' = picture of Prince Charles! Pupils have to guess which person is 'speaking'.

✱ Give pairs of pupils some time to note down a similar description of one of the other personalities. They then read their description for the class to guess.

✱ Pupils fill in sheet 18a without their names. The sheets are then redistributed and pupils either read them individually to work out who wrote it, or read the descriptions to the class, who must put a name to the details.

✱ Pupils could also fill in sheet 18a, imagining that they are their favourite sports/ music star. Pictures from magazines and newspapers could be cut out to accompany these descriptions, making a good wall display.

✱ Pupils could present themselves on video and show this to a different year group at school.

✱ Using clips of TV characters, encourage pupils to speak from visual prompts about the character as if that person were speaking, eg 'The Simpsons' – 'Ich heiße Bart. Ich habe zwei Schwestern. Ich habe gelbe Haare' etc.

Further activities

✱ Pupils could set up a 'Blind Date' show where three contestants describe themselves and the fourth must ask two or three questions about them using ideas from units in the course, eg 'Hast du ein Tier?' or 'Magst du Schokolade?' They then have to choose one of the three who have given the answers for a 'blind date'. The pupils could dress up and use this as a prompt to talk about their clothes, pretend to be from another country or need everything to be spelled out for them. The language use is endless!

Mein persönliches Informationsblatt

My personal information sheet

Ich heiße _____.

Ich bin _____ Jahre alt.

Mein Geburtstag ist am _____.

Ich bin _____.

Ich habe _____ Bruder/Brüder. Ich habe keinen Bruder.
Ich habe _____ Schwester/n. Ich habe keine Schwester.

Ich wohne in _____.
Ich wohne in einem _____.

Ich habe _____ Haare.
Ich habe _____ Augen.

Ich habe ein Tier. Ich habe _____.

Ich mag _____.
Ich mag _____ nicht.

In der Schule lerne ich _____ und _____.

Ich mag Deutsch und _____.
Ich mag Sport. Ich mag _____.

Ich trage _____.
Ich spreche Deutsch!

Das ist Deutsch!

© Kathy Williams and Amanda Doyle

Grammar Points

We are assuming a basic knowledge of German on the part of the teacher. The following is included as a general reminder only.

Definite and indefinite articles

Definite Articles (the)				
Case	**Masculine**	**Feminine**	**Neuter**	**Plural**
Nominative	der	die	das	die
Accusative	den	die	das	die
Dative	dem	der	dem	den
Genitive	des	der	des	der

Indefinite Articles (a/an)				
Case	**Masculine**	**Feminine**	**Neuter**	**Plural**
Nominative	ein	eine	ein	keine*
Accusative	einen	eine	ein	keine*
Dative	einem	einer	einem	keinen*
Genitive	eines	einer	eines	keiner*

* Note: keine is the negative of eine (which has no plural form), but keine (no/none) can be used in the plural: 'Er hat **keine** Bücher' (He has no books) or 'In Venedig gibt es **keine** Autos' (In Venice there are no cars).

Cases and adjectival endings

Nominative – the subject
Accusative – the direct object
Dative – the indirect object
Genitive – the possessive case, ie des = 'of the'

Nominative Case (Subject Case)			
Masculine der der neu**e** Wagen the new car	**Feminine** die die schön**e** Stadt the beautiful city	**Neuter** das das alt**e** Auto the old car	**Plural** die die neu**en** Bücher the new books
Masculine ein ein neu**er** Wagen a new car	**Feminine** eine eine schön**e** Stadt a beautiful city	**Neuter** ein ein alt**es** Auto an old car	**Plural** keine keine neu**en** Bücher no new books

Accusative Case (Direct Object)			
Masculine den den neu**en** Wagen the new car	**Feminine** die die schön**e** Stadt the beautiful city	**Neuter** das das alt**e** Auto the old car	**Plural** die die neu**en** Bücher the new books
Masculine einen einen neu**en** Wagen a new car	**Feminine** eine eine schön**e** Stadt a beautiful city	**Neuter** ein ein alt**es** Auto an old car	**Plural** keine keine neu**en** Bücher no new books

Das ist Deutsch!

Dative Case (Indirect Object)			
Masculine dem dem nett**en** Mann (to) the nice man	**Feminine** der der schön**en** Frau (to) the beautiful woman	**Neuter** dem dem nett**en** Mädchen (to) the nice girl	**Plural** den den ander**en** Leuten* (to) the other people
Masculine einem einem nett**en** Mann (to) a nice man	**Feminine** einer einer schön**en** Frau (to) a beautiful woman	**Neuter** einem einem nett**en** Mädchen (to) a nice girl	**Plural** keinen keinen ander**en** Leuten* (to) no other people

* Plural nouns in the dative add an -n or -en ending if the plural form does not already end in -(e)n.

NOTE: The endings of the adjective are the same in Genitive and Dative, but not the endings of the nouns and the article. Only in feminine words are they all the same: Das Auto eines netten Mannes (The car of a nice man).

Schlüsselwörter – Key words

A

abschreiben	to copy
acht	8
achtundzwanzig	28
achtzehn	18
die Adresse	address
meine Adresse ist	my address is
Alles Gute zum Geburtstag!	Happy Birthday!
die Äpfel (m pl)	apples
April (m)	April
arbeiten	to work
der Arm	arm
das Auge	eye
die Augen	eyes
aufstehen	to stand up
auf Wiedersehen	goodbye
August (m)	August
ausfüllen	to fill in
das Auto	car
mit dem Auto	by car

B

das Badezimmer	bathroom
der Bahnhof	station (bus/train)
die Bank	bank
beantworten	to answer
das Bein	leg
in die Berge	to the mountains
das Bett	bed
bitte	please
blau	blue
bleiben	to stay
der Bleistift	pencil
der Bleistiftspitzer	sharpener
blond	blond
braun	brown
das Brot	bread
der Bruder	brother
der Bus	bus
mit dem Bus	by bus
die Butter	butter

C

das Café	café

die Cola	Coke

D

der Dachboden	loft
Däne	Danishman
Dänemark (n)	Denmark
Dänin	Danishwoman
danke	thank you
das (n)	the
das ist	it is/this is
das macht 50 Euros	that comes to 50 Euros
das sind	these are
das Denkmal	monument
der (m)	the
Deutsch (n)	German (language)
die Deutsche	German woman
der Deutsche	German man
Deutschland (n)	Germany
Dezember (m)	December
die (f)	the
die Diele	the hall
Dienstag (m)	Tuesday
Donnerstag (m)	Thursday
dort	there
drei	3
dreißig	30
dreiundzwanzig	23
dreizehn	13
da drüben	over there

E

Ein gutes neues Jahr!	Happy New Year!
eins	1
einunddreißig	31
einundzwanzig	21
elf	11
England (n)	England
der Engländer	Englishman
die Engländerin	Englishwoman
Englisch (n)	English (language)
entschuldigung	excuse me
er ist/sie ist/es ist … (m/f/n)	It is …

Das ist Deutsch!

es (n)	it
es gibt … (plus accusative)	there is/are
es ist … Uhr	it is … o'clock
ich esse	I eat
essen	to eat
das Essen	food
das Esszimmer	dining room

F

ich fahre …	I am going …
fahren	to go
das Fahrrad	bicycle
mit dem Fahrrad	by bicycle
die Fahrt	journey
Februar (m)	February
das Federmäppchen	pencil case
der Feiertag	holiday
fertig	ready/finished
fertig machen	to complete/ finish
finden	to find
der Fisch	fish
das Flugzeug	plane
mit dem Flugzeug	by plane
Frankreich (n)	France
der Franzose	Frenchman
die Französin	Frenchwoman
Freitag (m)	Friday
die Freizeit	free time
Frohe Ostern!	Happy Easter!
Fröhliche Weihnachten!	Merry Christmas!
im Frühling	in spring
fünf	5
fünfundzwanzig	25
fünfzehn	15
der Fuß	foot
zu Fuß	on foot

G

die Garage	garage
der Geburtstag	birthday
mein Geburtstag	my birthday
ich gehe	I go/walk
Geisteswissenschaften (pl)	humanities
gelb	yellow
die Geschwister	siblings

grau	grey
groß	big
grün	green
gut	good/fine
Gut, danke	Fine, thank you
Gute Fahrt!	Safe journey!
Guten Tag	hello

H

die Haare	hair
Ich habe … (plus accusative)	I have …
haben	to have
Haben Sie eine Wahl getroffen?	Have you made your choice?
die Hand	hand
das Haus	house
nach Hause	(to go) home
ich komme nach Hause	I arrive home
zu Hause	at home
die Haustiere	pets
das Heft	exercise book
heiß	hot
es ist heiß	it is hot
Ich heiße …	my name is …
heißen	to be named
im Herbst	in autumn
heute	today
hier	here
Holländer	Dutchman
Holländerin	Dutchwoman
ich höre	I listen
höre zu	listen
das Hörnchen	croissant
die Hose	trousers
der Hot Dog	hot dog
das Hotel	hotel
der Hund	dog
der Hut	hat

I

die Informatik	ICT
in/im	in
interessant	interesting
der Ire	Irish man
die Irin	Irish woman
Irland (n)	Ireland

ist …	is …
Italien (n)	Italy
der Italiener	Italian man
die Italienerin	Italian woman

J

ja	yes
Januar (m)	January
die Jeans	jeans
Juli (m)	July
Juni (m)	June

K

der Kaffee	coffee
kalt	cold
es ist kalt	it is cold
das Kaninchen	rabbit
die Kartoffelchips	crisps
der Käse	cheese
das Käsesandwich	cheese sandwich
die Katze	cat
kein/keine	no/none
der Keller	cellar
die Kirche	church
das Kleid	dress
der Kleiderschrank	wardrobe
klein	small
das Knie	knee
der Kopf	head
die Krawatte	tie
die Küche	kitchen
der Kuchen	cake
die Kunst	art
der Kugelschreiber	pen
kurz	short

L

aufs Land	to the countryside
lang	long
langweilig	boring
(vor)lesen	to read (out)
lila	purple
das Lineal	ruler
links	left

M

Ich mache …	I do … (+ activity)
machen	to do
Ich mag …	I like …
Ich mag kein(e) …	I don't like …
Ich mag … nicht	I don't like …
der Magen	stomach
Magst du … ?	Do you like … ?
Mai (m)	May
der Mantel	coat
März (m)	March
die Mathe	maths
die Maus	mouse
ans Meer	to the seaside
das Meerschweinchen	guinea pig
mein/meine	my
das Mineralwasser	mineral water
am Mittag	at midday
um Mitternacht	at midnight
Mittwoch (m)	Wednesday
Ich möchte …	I would like …
Möchtes du etwas … ?	Would you like some … ?
die Monate des Jahres	the months of the year
Montag (m)	Monday
der Mund	mouth
das Museum	museum
die Musik	music
die Mutter	mother
meine Mutter	my mother
der Muttertag	Mother's Day

N

nach	to/after
die Nase	nose
die Nationalflagge von …	the national flag of …
die Naturwissenschaft	science
nein	no
das Neujahr	New Year
neun	9
neunundzwanzig	29
neunzehn	19
die Niederlande (n pl)	The Netherlands
im Norden	in the north
das Nordirland	Northern Ireland
November (m)	November
die Nummer	number

Das ist Deutsch!   © Kathy Williams and Amanda Doyle

O

die Ohren	ears
Oktober (m)	October
orange	orange
im Osten	in the east
das Ostern	Easter
Österreich (n)	Austria
Österreich	Austrian man
Österreichin	Austrian woman

P

der Parkplatz	car park
die Party	party
das Pferd	horse
zu Pferd	by horse
die Pizza	pizza
Polen (n)	Poland
Polen	Polish man
Polin	Polish woman
die Polizeiwache	police station
die Pommes Frites	chips
das Postamt	post office

R

der Radiergummi	eraser
rechts	right
ich rede	I talk
es regnet	it rains/is raining
der Rock	skirt
rosa	pink
rot	red

S

der Saft	fruit juice
Samstag (m)	Saturday
das Sandwich	sandwich
schau hin	watch/look
das Schiff	ship
mit dem Schiff	by ship
der Schinken	ham
das Schinkensandwich	ham sandwich
das Schlafzimmer	bedroom
es schneit	it snows/is snowing
die Schokolade	chocolate
es ist schön	it is fine
der Schotte	Scottish man

die Schottin	Scottish woman
Schottland (n)	Scotland
schrecklich	awful
schreiben	to write
die Schuhe	shoes
die Schule	school
die Schulter	shoulder
die Schuluniform	school uniform
schwarz	black
die Schweiz (f)	Switzerland
Schweizer	Swiss man
Schweizerin	Swiss woman
(zu) schwer	(too) difficult
die Schwester	sister
das Schwimmbad	swimming pool
sechs	6
sechsundzwanzig	26
sechzehn	16
sehen	to see
ich sehe fern	I watch TV
sehr gut	very good
September (m)	September
setzen, bitte	sit down, please (whole class)
setz dich, bitte	sit down, please (one person)
die Shorts	shorts
sieben	7
siebenundzwanzig	27
siebzehn	17
das Silvester	New Year's Eve
die Socken	socks
im Sommer	in summer
es ist sonnig	it is sunny
Sonntag (m)	Sunday
Spanien (n)	Spain
der Spanier	Spanish man
die Spanierin	Spanish woman
ich spiele	I play
die Spinne	spider
der Sport	sport
sprecht mir nach	say after me (whole class)
sprich mir nach	say after me (one person)
der Stuhl	chair
mein Stundenplan (m)	my timetable
im Süden	in the south
der Supermarkt	supermarket
süß	cute/sweet

T

die Tafel	table
die Tage (m pl)	the days
die Tage der Woche	the days of the week
die Tasche	bag
der Tee	tea
der Teppich	rug
die Tiere	animals
toll	great
ich trage	I wear/I am wearing
das T-shirt	T-shirt
die Turnschuhe	trainers

V

verbinden	to join
mein Vater	my father
der Vatertag	Father's Day
vier	4
vierundzwanzig	24
vierzehn	14
der Vogel	bird

W

Wales (n)	Wales
der Waliser	Welsh man
die Waliserin	Welsh woman
wann?	when?
Was ist es?	What is it?
das Weihnachten	Christmas
weiß	white
Welche Farbe ... ?	What colour ... ?
Wer ist das?	Who is it?
im Westen	in the west
das Wetter	weather
Wie alt bist du?	How old are you?
Wie geht's?	How are you?
Wie heißt du?	What is your name?
Wie ist das Wetter?	How is the weather?
es ist windig	it is windy
im Winter	in winter
Wo ist ... ?	Where is ... ?
Wo wohnst du?	Where do you live?
die Woche	week

Wohin fährst du?/ Wohin fahren Sie?	Where are you going?
Ich wohne in ...	I live in ...
das Wohnzimmer	living room
wunderbar	wonderful

Z

zehn	10
zeichnen	to draw
die Zitronenlimonade	lemonade
der Zug	train
mit dem Zug	by train
zwanzig	20
zwei	2
zweiundzwanzig	22
zwölf	12

Das ist Deutsch! © *Kathy Williams and Amanda Doyle*

Lightning Source UK Ltd.
Milton Keynes UK
UKOW02f0605140813

215343UK00002B/21/P